lonely planet

KT-170-325

Pocket
BRUGES & BRUSSELS

TOP SIGHTS • LOCAL LIFE • MADE EASY

Helena Smith

In This Book

QuickStart Guide

Your keys to understanding the cities – we help you decide what to do and how to do it

Need to Know
Tips for a smooth trip

Neighbourhoods
What's where

Explore Bruges & Brussels

The best things to see and do, neighbourhood by neighbourhood

Top Sights
Make the most of your visit

Local Life
The insider's city

The Best of Bruges & Brussels

The cities' highlights in handy lists to help you plan

Best Walks
See the city on foot

Bruges & Brussels' Best...
The best experiences

Survival Guide

Tips and tricks for a seamless, hassle-free experience in Bruges and Brussels

Getting Around
Travel like a local

Essential Information
Including where to stay

Our selection of the cities' best places to eat, drink and experience:

◎ Sights

✖ Eating

🍷 Drinking

★ Entertainment

🅰 Shopping

These symbols give you the vital information for each listing:

- 📞 Telephone Numbers
- 🕐 Opening Hours
- 🅿 Parking
- 🚭 Nonsmoking
- @ Internet Access
- 🛜 Wi-Fi Access
- 🥗 Vegetarian Selection
- 📖 English-Language Menu

- 👪 Family-Friendly
- 🐾 Pet-Friendly
- 🚌 Bus
- ⛴ Ferry
- Ⓜ Metro
- Ⓢ Subway
- 🚋 Tram
- 🚆 Train

Find each listing quickly on maps for each neighbourhood:

Bar Hemingway

16 🍷 Map p233, B2

Legend has it that Hemi[n]... self, wielding a machine[gun]... [libe]rate this timber-pan[elled]... [cent]ered bar during... [The] showpiece is a... [driv]en by Papa a[nd]... town. Dress... s.com; Hôtel Rit[z]... 🕐 6.30pm-2a[m]

Lonely Planet's
Bruges & Brussels

Lonely Planet Pocket Guides are designed to get you straight to the heart of the destination.

Inside you'll find all the must-see sights, plus tips to make your visit to each one really memorable. We've split the cities into easy-to-navigate neighbourhoods and provided clear maps so you'll find your way around with ease. Our expert authors have searched out the best of the cities: walks, food, nightlife and shopping, to name a few. Because you want to explore, our 'Local Life' pages will take you to some of the most exciting areas to experience the real Bruges and Brussels.

And of course you'll find all the practical tips you need for a smooth trip: itineraries for short visits, how to get around, and how much to tip the guy who serves you a drink at the end of a long day's exploration.

It's your guarantee of a really great experience.

Our Promise

You can trust our travel information because Lonely Planet authors visit the places we write about, each and every edition. We never accept freebies for positive coverage, so you can rely on us to tell it like it is.

QuickStart Guide 7

Explore Bruges & Brussels 21

The Best of Bruges & Brussels 127

Bruges & Brussels' Best Walks

Bruges & Brussels' Best...

Survival Guide 153

QuickStart Guide

Welcome to Bruges & Brussels

Romantic, canal-woven Bruges and buzzing multinational Brussels are both unmissable. While Brussels dwarfs Bruges in size, both feature boats plying waterways, serene parks, a web of cycling trails, jumbled market stalls, forward-looking fashion and galleries packed with home-grown art, from Brueghel masterpieces to Hergé's Tintin. All this, plus the finest beer and chocolate in the world.

Canal scene (p34), Bruges
BOTOND HORVATH/SHUTTERSTOCK ©

👁 Bruges & Brussels
Top Sights

Grand Place (p66)

The core of the Belgian capital, and quite simply the most theatrical medieval square in Europe, with a magnificent array of gabled guildhouses and a spectacular town hall.

Markt (p24)

The beating heart of Bruges, dominated by a high bell tower and artfully lit at night. Take a trip in a horse and carriage from here, or climb the tower to get a bird's eye view of the stunningly pretty city.

Burg (p26)

Gorgeously gaudy buildings, decorated with shining gilt and clusters of statues. A basilica with a holy relic allegedly containing Christ's blood draws both local Bruges worshippers and tourists.

Musée Horta (p120)

When Horta designed his house in Brussels, he combined technological innovation with high artistry to create a stunning, poetic, art nouveau masterpiece. It's worth seeing just for the wonderful twirling staircase.

Groeningemuseum (p46)

A potted history of Belgian art, with an outstanding collection of works by the Flemish Primitives, as well as cityscapes depicting Belgium in its Golden Age and surrealist pieces by Hieronymous Bosch.

Musée des Instruments de Musique (p92)

Inside one of Brussels' most spectacular art nouveau buildings, this museum takes you on a wonderful audio tour of world music, with umpteen arcane instruments on display.

Memlingmuseum (p48)

An unmissable Bruges sight, this small collection of devotional paintings and portraits glows in the dim light of an ancient hospital chapel. The gilded reliquary of St Ursula is an especial highlight.

Begijnhof (p50)

Once a retreat for single and widowed women, don't miss this absorbing house museum where you can wander through the rustic interior, or take a turn under the tall trees around the tranquil courtyard.

Centre Belge de la Bande Dessinée (p68)

Within this department store is a temple to Belgian and international cartoons. Pride of place goes to Hergé's beloved Tintin, but you'll also find Hokusai cartoons and manga.

Musées Royaux des Beaux-Arts (p90)

Brussels' major gallery covers everything from early Flemish painting to surrealist master Magritte, don't miss Brueghel's *Fall of Icarus* and Hans Memling's elegant portraits.

Parc du Cinquantenaire (p108)

The EU district boasts this spacious and leafy park, ringed by impressive museums including a military museum and one dedicated solely to cars.

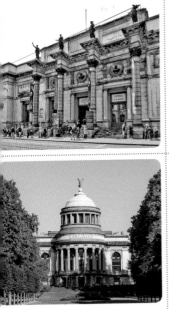

Musée du Cinquantenaire (p110)

Impressive if a little daunting, this museum has pretty much everything covered, from prehistoric wonders to Egyptian sarcophagi to the swirly splendours of art nouveau.

Belgian Coast (p62)

Belgium's coast features long sandy strands and low-key resort towns such as Ostend, as well as sights and memorials associated with the world wars.

Bruges & Brussels
Local Life

Insider tips to help you find the real city

Bruges gets a bad rap for being tourist central, but we've located tempting local shops and charming crowd-free back streets. Plus, in Brussels, we lead you to hip designer fashion and flea and food markets.

Shop Local, Central Bruges (p28)

▶ Obscure beers
▶ Vintage lace

Avid shoppers will find real gems in Bruges, where you can purchase everything from artisanal cheese to homemade *jenever* (ginlike drink) to antique crockery. Belgium's famous fashion designers get a look in too. The stunning Markt hosts a food market every Wednesday.

St-Anna Windmills, Bruges (p30)

▶ Windmills
▶ Folk museum

Escape the crowds in Bruges: a gentle wander northeast of the centre reveals a remarkable church, a folk museum, lace-marking project, four windmills and a venerable pub.

A Stroll in the Marolles, Brussels (p122)

▶ Markets
▶ Local restaurants

Working-class Brussels lives on in the intriguing Marolles district. At the Gare du Midi market see how immigration is shaping the city, while at the Jeu-de-Balle flea market you can pick up quirky antiques.

Shopping in Ste-Catherine, Brussels (p124)

▶ Cutting-edge fashion
▶ Live jazz

Belgian designers are known worldwide for their cutting-edge approach, and Rue Antoine Dansaert and the surrounding streets make up Brussels' fashion district.

Markt (p24) cafes

Shopper on Rue Antoine Dansaert

Other great places to experience the cities like a local:

Late-Night Eating, Bruges (p36)

De Republiek, Bruges (p38)

Vintage, Bruges (p58)

Mokafé, Brussels (p74)

Aux Armes de Bruxelles, Brussels (p78)

Jazz in Brussels (p85)

Recyclart, Brussels (p96)

Maison Antoine, Brussels (p115)

Bruges & Brussels
Day Planner

Day One, Bruges

Stroll past the colonnaded **fish market** (p42) and along the famous canals, or see the city from the water by taking a half-hour **canal cruise** (p53). Get a bird's-eye view of Bruges by climbing to the top of the **Belfort** (p25), then descend to visit the holiest relic in town in the **Heilig-Bloedbasiliek** (p27), before joining the locals lunching at **De Belegde Boterham** (p29).

Admire Belgian art from the Flemish Primitives to the surrealists at the **Groeningemuseum** (p46) and take time out in the courtyard of the serene **begijnhof** (p50), making sure to visit the little house museum there. Tour **Brouwerij De Halve Maan** (p55), where Brugse Zot is created: you'll get to taste a beer sample en route.

Continue the beer theme with a meal at classy **Den Dyjver** (p56), where beer is not only paired with each dish, but is also a key ingredient in the cooking. For yet more Belgian brews, head below ground to tucked-away cellar bar **'t Poatersgat** (p39), or wander the back streets to find the city's oldest pub, picturesque **Herberg Vlissinghe** (p39).

Day Two, Bruges

Steer away from the tourist centre and take a morning stroll around the St-Anna district, visiting the **Jeruzalemkerk** (p34), the **'t Apostelientje** (p31) lace shop, **Museum voor Volkskunde** (p30) and the **four windmills** (p31), which enjoy a stately position on a verdant bank. Stop for a pub lunch and a *gueuze* (lambic beers) at **De Windmolen** (p31).

Head back to the centre for an artistic highlight of the city: the **Hans Memling paintings** (p4) in the chapel of a medieval hospital; with the same ticket you see the museum's characterful tiled pharmacy. Escape the crowds again and have a wander in the **Minnewater Park** (p131), before stopping for a drink at local favourite **De Stoepa** (p56).

Have dinner at lively bistro **L'Estaminet** (p29), then catch a classical concert at the modern **Concertgebouw** (p58), or see a movie at art-house **Cinema Lumière** (p41). Afterwards, head next door for a drink at lively **De Republiek** (p38), which is always packed with young Bruges-dwellers.

Short on time?
We've arranged Bruges & Brussels' must-sees into these day-by-day itineraries to make sure you see the very best of the cities in the time you have available.

Day Three, Brussels

The gilded facades encircling Brussels' splendid **Grand Place** (p66) glint in the early morning sun, making it a picturesque spot to kick off a tour of the capital. While here, pop into the city's history museum, **Brussels City Museum** (p74), then stroll through the glass-roofed **Galeries St-Hubert** (p75) to Brussels' **cathedral** (p96) and towards the museums.

Once in the Mont des Arts area, time your trip to the **Musée des Instruments de Musique** (p92) for lunch at its rooftop *café* (pub), housed in a tall and spectacular art nouveau building. If you've got the energy, check out the **Musée BELvue** (p98) for a dose of Brussels history and the **Musées Royaux des Beaux-Arts** (p90), which showcases Belgian art, from the Flemish Primitives via Brueghel to Magritte.

Head downhill for dinner and jazz at **Le Cercle des Voyageurs** (p76). Alternatively, take the glass lift outside the colossal **Palais de Justice** (p97) to the Marolles area to dine at one of its renowned restaurants – try **L'Idiot du Village** (p123).

Day Four, Brussels

Browse the **Belgian designer boutiques** (p125) along Rue Antoine Dansaert and the surrounding streets, which showcase big names and hot new talents. Then continue the sartorial theme by heading to the little-known but absorbing costume and lace museum: **Musée du Costume et de la Dentelle** (p72).

Either hop on the tram to Victor Horta's gorgeous art nouveau home-turned-museum, the **Musée Horta** (p121), or instead take the metro east and visit the museums of the EU district, of which the **Musée du Cinquantenaire** (p110) are the standouts, with rich collections of antiquities. Have a stroll round leafy **Parc du Cinquantenaire** (p108) before heading back to town for classic waffles, sprinkled with icing sugar, at **Mokafé** (p74).

Start your evening with a half-and-half at **Le Cirio** (p78) before taking in a traditional puppet show at the quaint **Théâtre Royal de Toone** (p83), or listening to some live music at the **Music Village** (p82). If neither of these options appeals, try a classical concert at Horta-designed **BOZAR** (p103).

Need to Know

**For more information,
see Survival Guide (p153)**

Currency
The euro (€)

Language
French and Dutch

Visas
Not required for US, Canadian, Australian,
New Zealand or South African visitors for
stays up to six months. European Union
nationals can stay indefinitely.

Money
ATMs are widespread. Cash preferred in
small shops; major credit cards in
larger ones.

Mobile Phones
European and Australian mobile phones will
work. US visitors should check with their
service provider. Buy a local SIM card to
bring costs down.

Time
Central European Time (GMT/UTC plus
one hour)

Plugs & Adaptors
Two-pin plugs; current is 220V. North
American visitors require adaptors.

Tipping
Not obligatory, as service charges and Value
Added Tax (VAT) are included in hotel and
restaurant prices. It's common to round up
restaurant bills and taxi fares by a euro or two.

① Before You Go

Your Daily Budget

Budget less than €60
- Dorm bed €25–€35
- Supermarkets and set-price lunchtime specials
- Free national museums, church concerts

Midrange €60–€150
- Double room €90
- Two-course dinner with glass of wine €30
- Jazz concert ticket €15

Top End more than €150
- four-star hotel double room €200
- Three-course dinner in top restaurant with wine €60
- Ticket to classical-music concert at BOZAR €65

Useful Websites

Lonely Planet (www.lonelyplanet.com) Great for planning.

Agenda (www.agenda.be) Nightlife and exhibitions: look out for the trilingual print version too.

Visit Brussels (visitbrussels.be) Slick and super-helpful tourist-board site.

Advance Planning

One month Book accommodation early, particularly for Bruges in high season.

Two weeks Book a Brussels Greeter (www.brussels.greeters.be) for insider insight.

A few days Buy concert tickets online.

2 Arriving in Bruges & Brussels

ost travellers to Belgium, whether arriv-
g by air or rail, will generally arrive first in
ussels and then catch onward transport
Bruges.

Arriving by Air

ussels International Airport (www.
usselsairport.be) is situated 14km north-
st of the city. There are regular trains and
ses into central Brussels, from where you
n catch onward trains to Bruges.

ussels South Charleroi Airport (www.
arleroi-airport.com), Brussels' second
port, is 46km southeast of the city and
used mainly by budget airlines including
yanair. From here, you can catch buses to
oth Brussels and Bruges.

Arriving by Train

ruxelles-Midi (South Station) is the main
ation for international connections: Euro-
ar, TGV and Thalys high-speed trains only
op here. Take the metro or a taxi from Midi
the centre of town.

ost other mainline trains stop at **Bruxelles-
idi** (Gare du Midi), **Bruxelles-Central** (Gare
entrale, Central Station) and, except for
msterdam trains, also at **Bruxelles-Nord**
Gare du Nord, North Station).

egular trains from Brussels to **Bruges**
epart hourly from all three main stations
Bruxelles-Midi, Bruxelles-Central and
ruxelles-Nord).

3 Getting Around

Bruges

Bruges' train station is 1.5km south of Markt;
from here you can catch a taxi or bus into
town, or take a scenic 20-minute walk.

Car

Given central Bruges' one-way system, it's best
to use the large covered car park (per hour/
24-hours €0.50/2.50) beside the train station.

Taxi

Taxis wait on the Markt and in front of the
train station. Otherwise phone 📞 050 33 44
44 or 📞 050 38 46 60.

Brussels

Brussels' integrated bus-tram-metro system
runs from 6am to midnight, except on Friday
and Saturday, when 17 Noctis night-bus
routes operate twice hourly from midnight to
3am, most starting from Place de Brouckère.

M Metro, Tram & Bus

Lines 1A (northwest–southeast) and 1B
(northeast–southwest) share the same
central stretch. Underground premetro trams
also link Bruxelles-Nord with Bruxelles-Midi
via the Bourse.

STIB/MIVB tickets are valid across all
services – tickets must be validated before
travel in machines located at the entrance to
metro stations, or inside trams and buses.

Taxi

In Brussels, official taxis charge €2.40 plus
pick-up €1.80/2.70 per kilometre within/
outside the Brussels region. There's a €2 supplement between 10pm and 6am. Taxes and
tips are officially included in the meter price.

Bicycle

Villo! (en.villo.be) is a system of 180 automated stations for short-term bicycle rental
in Brussels.

Bruges
Neighbourhoods

Burg, Markt & the North (p22)
Two stunning interlinked squares are the perfect introduction to the medieval city, and the surrounding lanes are delightful for exploring.

◉ Top Sights

Markt

Burg

Groeningemuseum & the South (p44)
Bruges' major museums are here, including standout collections of the Flemish Primitives, while the Begijnhof is a green retreat.

◉ Top Sights

Groeningemuseum

Memlingmuseum

Begijnhof

Worth a Trip

◉ Top Sights

Belgian Coast (p62)

◉ Markt
◉ Burg
◉ Groeningemuseum
◉ Memlingmuseum
◉ Begijnhof

Brussels
Neighbourhoods

Parc du Cinquantenaire & EU Quarter (p106)

As well as being the gleaming centre of EU power, this district boasts a beautiful park and some fine museums.

◉ Top Sights

Parc du Cinquantenaire

Musée du Cinquantenaire

Grand Place & Îlot Sacré (p64)

The geographical heart of Brussels, with dazzling medieval buildings and standout restaurants, theatres and music venues.

◉ Top Sights

Grand Place

Centre Belge de la Bande Dessinée

Worth a Trip

◉ Top Sights

Musée Horta (p120)

Worth a Trip

◯ Local Life

The Marolles (p122)

Ste-Catherine (p124)

Centre Belge de la Bande Dessinée

Grand Place

Musée des Instruments de Musique

Parc du Cinquantenaire

Musées Royaux des Beaux-Arts

Musée du Cinquantenaire

Musée Horta

Royal Quarter Museums (p88)

This stately district has a compelling cluster of museums, some lovely green spaces, and the city's best chocolatiers.

◉ Top Sights

Musées Royaux des Beaux-Arts

Musée des Instruments de Musique

Bruges

★ BRUSSELS

BELGIUM

| 0 | 150 km |
| 0 | 100 miles |

Explore
Bruges

Explore
Brussels

Worth a Trip

Outdoor cafes, Brussels
SYLVAIN SONNET/GETTY IMAGES©

Explore

Burg, Markt & the North

If you set out to design a fairy-tale medieval town it would be hard to improve on central Bruges. Picturesque cobbled lanes and dreamy canals link photogenic market squares lined with soaring towers and historic churches. The only downside is the crush of tourists, especially in summer. Wander to the north and east of the centre, though, and you'll discover a different, more enigmatic Bruges.

The Sights in a Day

☀ Start with a coffee on the **Markt** (p24), then climb the **Belfort** (p25) to get your bearings on the city and beyond. Head to the **Burg** (p26), exploring the Renaissancezaal (Renaissance Hall) within the **Brugse Vrije** (p27), and deciphering the colourful murals of the Gotische Zaal (Gothic Hall) in the **Stadhuis** (p27). Then see the city's most sacred relic, housed in the **Heilig-Bloedbasiliek** (p27). For lunch, sample the wares at one of the two *frites* (chips) sellers on the Markt.

☀ Nearby, the grandiose **Koninklijke Stadsschouwburg** (p41) is a handsome 19th-century theatre, while to the east in tranquil St-Anna you'll find the ghoulishly intriguing 15th-century **Jeruzalemkerk** (p34), with its skull-bedecked altarpiece.

☾ For more immersion in old Bruges, have a hearty supper and a beer at **Herberg Vlissinghe** (p39), a fixture since 1515. Quintessential Bruges beer experiences can also be had at cellar bar **'t Poatersgat** (p39). Finally, return to the Markt to see the square in all its floodlit glory.

For a local's day in Bruges, see p28 and p30.

⊙ Top Sights

◯ Local Life

♥ Best of Bruges

Drinking Beer

Markets

Getting There

🚆 **Train** From the station it takes around 20 minutes to walk to the centre of Bruges.

🚌 **Bus** Any bus marked 'Centrum' runs to the Markt.

Top Sights
Markt

Flanked by medieval-style step-gabled buildings, this wonderfully dramatic open market square is Bruges' nerve centre. Horse-drawn carriages clatter between open-air restaurants and camera-clicking tourists, watched over by a statue of Pieter De Coninck and Jan Breydel, the leaders of the Bruges Matins. It's undeniably one of the most touristy parts of town, but visually it's stunning and shouldn't be missed; there's more of a local feel on Wednesday when a food market takes centre stage.

Map p32, B7

Medieval houses in Markt

Don't Miss

The Belfort

The symbol of Bruges is its Unesco-listed 13th-century **belfry** (adult/child €8/5; ⏱9.30am-5pm, last tickets 4.15pm), rising a lofty 83m above the Markt. Ascending the 366 steps brings you past the treasury, a triumphal bell and a 47-bell manually operated carillon, which still regularly chimes across the city. Once at the top, look out across the spires and red-tiled rooftops towards the wind turbines and giant cranes of Zeebrugge. Visitor numbers are limited to 70 at once, which can cause queues at peak times.

Historium

The **Historium** (www.historium.be; Markt 1; adult/child €11/5.50; ⏱10am-6pm) occupies a fine neo-Gothic building on the northern side of the square. Taking visitors back to 1435, it is an immersive multi-media experience, claiming to be more a medieval movie than a museum: you can survey the old port or watch Van Eyck paint. It's a little light on facts, so for many it will be a diversion from the real sights of the city, perhaps best for entertaining kids on a rainy day. A real-life beer *café* (pub) provides refreshments and views of the Markt.

The Market

Appropriately enough, this historic market square is still the location for a major food market held on Wednesday mornings. Locals and tourist mix to purchase cheeses, sausages, spit-roasted meat, fruit, veg and plants. Authentic waffles are sold from a van, and the Belfort looms picturesquely over proceedings.

The Eiermarkt

Immediately to the north and adjoining the Markt, this little square can be identified by a stone column surmounted by lions. It's ringed by *cafés* and bars, and is a marginally cheaper and less frenetic place for a coffee or a drink than the Markt itself.

☑ Top Tips

▸ If you're visiting lots of sights, consider buying a Bruges City Card (p159).

▸ Be sure to visit the square at night, when it's quieter and beautifully floodlit.

▸ Carriage tours (€39 for up to five people) depart from the Markt and take 30 minutes, including a pit stop at the *begijnhof* (p50).

▸ In summer, aim to make a carriage trip between 6pm and 7pm when most day-trippers have left town and Bruges' buildings glow golden in the sun's late rays.

✕ Take a Break

There are numerous tourist-orientated *cafés* to choose from on the square, or go for takeaway *frites* (from €2.25) and hot dogs (from €3) sold from two green vans on the Markt.

Top Sights
Burg

One short block east of the Markt, the less theatrical but still enchanting Burg has been Bruges' administrative hub for centuries. It also hosted the St Donatian Cathedral till 1799, when it was torn down by anti-religious zealots. A modern addition is the mildly baffling Toyo Ito pavilion, a geometric contemporary artwork at the square's tree-filled centre. With your back to it you can admire the southern flank of the Burg, incorporating three superb interlinked facades that glow with gilded detail.

Map p32, C7

Heilig-Bloedbasiliek

Don't Miss

Brugse Vrije

This wonderfully eye-catching building, with early baroque gabling and golden statuettes, was once the palace of the 'Liberty of Bruges', the large autonomous territory that was ruled from Bruges from 1121 to 1794. The building still houses city offices, but you can visit the **Renaissancezaal** (Renaissance Hall; Burg 11a; admission free; ☺9.30am-noon & 1.30-4.30pm) to admire its remarkable 1531 carved chimney piece.

Stadhuis

The beautiful 1420 **Stadhuis** (City Hall; Burg 12; admission free) has a fanciful facade covered with replica statues of the counts and countesses of Flanders (the originals were torn down in 1792 by French soldiers). Inside, an audioguide explains numerous portraits before leading you upstairs to the astonishing **Gotische Zaal** (Gothic Hall; adult/concession €4/3; ☺9.30am-5pm). Few rooms anywhere achieve such a jaw-dropping first impression as this dazzling hall with its polychrome ceiling, hanging vaults and romantic historical murals.

Heilig-Bloedbasiliek

The Stadhuis' western end morphs into the **Heilig-Bloedbasiliek** (Basilica of the Holy Blood; www.holyblood.com; Burg 5; admission €2; ☺9.30am-noon & 2-5pm, closed Wed afternoons mid-Nov–Mar), which takes its name from a phial supposedly containing a few drops of Christ's blood that was brought here after the Crusades. The right-hand door leads upstairs to a colourful chapel where the relic is hidden behind a flamboyant silver tabernacle. Also upstairs is the basilica's treasury, where you'll see the jewel-studded reliquary in which the phial is mounted on Ascension Day for the Heilig-Bloedprocessie.

☑ Top Tips

▶ Do take the (free) audioguide for the Gotische Zaal – it explains the narrative behind the murals and sheds light on the city's history.

▶ The Holy Blood relic in the basilica is brought out for veneration at 2pm daily – respectful and quiet visitors are welcome.

▶ Like the Markt, the Burg is at its most tranquil and beautiful in the early evening and at night.

▶ Just south of the Burg and across the bridge, don't miss the lovely colonnaded 1821 Vismarkt (p42), which still accommodates fish stalls most mornings, along with trinket sellers later in the day.

✕ Take a Break

Try tiny De Garre (p40), a beer lovers' favourite, tucked away on an alley between the Markt and the Burg.

Local Life
Shop Local in Central Bruges

There are times when central Bruges can feel like a melee of waffle stands and *frites* stalls. It's worth remembering, though, that this is indeed a real place, where discerning locals do their shopping, eating and drinking. Beyond the touristy facade, there are some real finds if you're looking for interesting beers, cheeses and charcuterie, as well as fashion, lace and bric-a-brac.

❶ Market Shop on the Markt
The Markt is, generally speaking, tourist central, crammed with horse carriages and tour groups. But on Wednesday mornings it's a genuinely local experience, when an excellent food market takes centre stage. It's ideal if you're planning a picnic, or simply want some fresh fruit to counter the heavy Belgian grub. Speciality cheeses and sausages are among the offerings.

2 Pick Up Fine Food at the Diksmuids Boterhuis

This gorgeously traditional **grocery** (www.diksmuidsboterhuis.be; Geldmuntstraat 23; ⏱10am-12.30pm & 2-6.30pm) now sits amid mainstream boutiques, but it's been here since 1933. Decked out with red and white gingham flounces and featuring a ceiling hung with sausages, it sells cheeses, honey, cold meat and mustard.

3 Women's Fashion at L'Heroine

The cool concrete exterior of **L'Heroine** (www.lheroine.be; Noordzandstraat 32; ⏱10.30am-6pm Mon-Sat) stands out among the chains. Here you'll find established Belgian designers Dries Van Noten and Ann Demeulemeester as well as young talents such as Christian Wijnants. They stock beautiful silk print dresses, asymmetrical tailoring and sumptuous scarves and drapes – staff can help you combine pieces for a strong, idiosyncratic look. It's less daunting than it looks, and you're welcome to browse.

4 Lunch at De Belegde Boterham

Duck the tourist crowds at this popular **lunch spot** (☎050 34 91 31; www.debelegdeboterham.be; Kleine St-Amandsstraat 5; mains from €12; ⏱noon-4pm Mon-Sat) for well-heeled locals. The monochrome boutique styling is a bit formal, but it's a friendly place and the food – soups, sandwiches and large salads – is excellent, with fresh ingredients and tasty dressings. Good coffee too.

5 Beer at Bacchus Cornelius

When locals buy run-of-the-mill beers – and chocolate – they do so at supermarkets. But if they want a special tipple, they come to **Bacchus Cornelius** (www.bacchuscornelius.com; Academiestraat 17; ⏱1-6.30pm). There's a cornucopia of 450 beers and rare *gueuzes*, as well as *jenevers* and liqueurs flavoured with elderflower, cranberries and cherries. Ask the shop owner if you can try her home-brewed silky smooth *jenever*, made with real chocolate. The two pianos are there for shoppers to play, and an open fire in winter adds to the cosy vibe.

6 Madam Mim for Bric-A-Brac

A must for lovers of vintage, adorable **Madam Mim** (www.madammim.be; Hoogstraat 29; ⏱11am-6pm Wed-Mon) sells quirky clothes handmade from vintage fabrics by shopowner Mim herself, as well as '60s crockery, cut glass, glorious hats and '70s kids' clothes. You can also pick up antique lace for a fraction of the cost it goes for elsewhere.

7 Dinner at L'Estaminet

With its weighty dark-timber beams, low lighting and convivial clatter, **L'Estaminet** (☎050 33 09 16; Park 5; beer/snacks/pastas from €1.80/6/8; ⏱11.30am-11pm Tue-Sun, 4-11pm Thu) – the name means tavern – scarcely seems to have changed since it opened in 1900. It's primarily a drinking spot, but also serves time-honoured dishes such as spaghetti bolognese with a baked cheese crust. Summer sees its loyal local following flow out onto the front terrace.

Local Life
St-Anna Windmills

The district of St-Anna provides a delightful breather away from central Bruges, as well as an insight into the industrious past of the district. The handmade lace industry is still just about alive – you can see lace being made at the Kantcentrum, while the folk museum explores the working lives of past residents. Four handsome windmills frame a spectacular vista over the town.

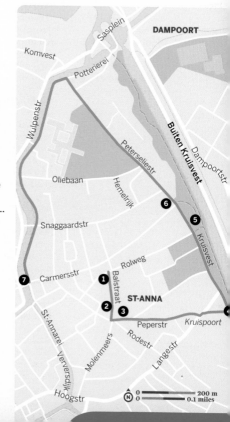

❶ **Visit the Museum voor Volkskunde**

This appealing **museum** (Museum of Folklore; Balstraat 43; adult/concession €4/3; ⊙9.30am-5pm Tue-Sun) presents visitors with 18 themed tableaux illustrating Flemish life in times gone by (a 1930s sweetshop, a hatter's workshop, a traditional kitchen etc). It's a static affair, but the setting is an attractive *godshuis* (alms-house) and the time-warp museum *café*, **De Zwarte Kat**, charges just €1.25 for a beer. Temporary exhibits upstairs are often worth a look.

2 Shop for lace at 't Apostelientje

Once you locate the scenic back-streets of Bruges you'll find there's scarcely a soul in sight. The delicate garments and gifts on sale at this quaint little **shop** (www.apostelientje. be; Balstraat 11; ⏱1-5pm Tue, 9.30am-12.15pm & 1.15-5pm Wed-Sat, 10am-1pm Sun) are made from beautiful and authentic lace, handmade by two sisters and their mother; the husband of one of the sisters makes the wooden bobbins. An unusual opportunity to buy the real Bruges deal lace-wise.

3 See Lace Created at the Kantcentrum

Past the dramatic Jeruzalemkerk, the **Kantcentrum** (Lace Centre; www. kantcentrum.com; Balstraat 16; adult/child €5/4; ⏱9:30am-5pm) displays a collection of lace in a row of interlinked old cottages. The centre's main attraction is that (afternoons only) you can watch bobbin lace being made by informal gatherings of experienced lace-makers and their students, who gather to chat and work here. Once you've seen how mind-bendingly fiddly the process is, you'll swiftly understand why handmade lace is so expensive.

4 View the Medieval Walls

The fortified gate-tower **Kruispoort** (on Langestraat) is an impressive iso-lated remnant of the former city wall.

5 Visit the Windmills

From the 13th century through to the 19th century, Bruges' ramparts were graced with *molens* (windmills); ambling along the canal bounding the eastern side of the city takes you through pretty parkland past Bruges' four remaining examples. The windmills still grind cereals into flour today, and two of the four – the 18th-century **St Janshuismolen** (Kruisvest; adult/concession €3/2; ⏱9.30am-12.30pm & 1.30-5pm Tue-Sun May-Sep), and the **Koeleweimolen** (Kruisvest; adult/concession €3/2; ⏱9.30am-12.30pm & 1.30-5pm Tue-Sun Jul & Aug) – house a little museum.

6 Break for a Drink at De Windmolen

Take a break at this quaint corner **café** (☎050 33 97 39; Carmersstraat 135; beer/snacks/pasta from €1.80/4.50/8.50; ⏱10am-late Mon-Thu, to 3am Fri & Sun), with a sunny terrace overlooking one of the St-Anna windmills. It's mainly patronised by locals, and offers a good low-key location to sample the local brews.

7 Follow Canalside Potterierei

Wind your way back to the centre along scenic Potterierei, where statues of the Madonna adorn every corner. Look out for the small lever bridge that's reminiscent of Amsterdam.

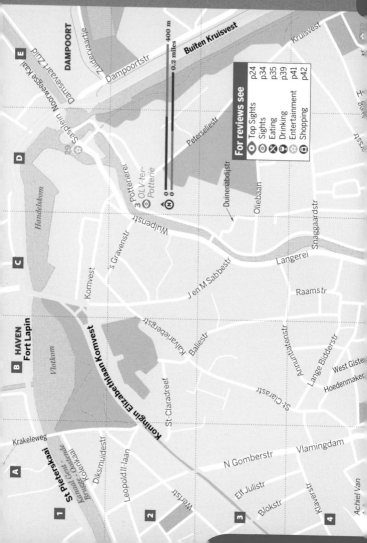

DAMPOORT

Buiten Kruisvest

For reviews see

◎	Top Sights	p24
◉	Sights	p34
✕	Eating	p35
✕	Drinking	p39
★	Entertainment	p41
⬛	Shopping	p42

400 m
0.2 miles

HAVEN
Fort Lapin

Koningin Elizabethlaan Komvest

ST-ANNA

Jeruzalemkerk

Balsemboomstr
Kwekersstr
Vuldersstr
Ganzestr
Kazernevest

Rodestr
Peperstr
Bilkske
Coupure

alstraat
Verbrand Nieuwland
Langestr
Predikherenrei
Schaarstr
Paardestraat
Gadel

De Damhouderstr
Blekersstr
St-Annarei
Molenmeers
Hoogstr
Predikherenstr
Groenerei
Peerdenstr
Engelstraat
Koningin Astridpark
Godshuis St-Trudo

Ververdijk
St-Maartens-plein
Boomgaardstr
Park
Freren Fonteinstr
Waalsestr
Suveestr Stalijzerstr
Eekhoutstr Garenmarkt

Gouden Handrei
Spiegelrei
Hoornstr
Koningstr
Engelsestr
Ridderstr
Twijnstr
Kelkstr
Crowne Plaza Hotel
't Pandreitje
Hof Arents

Woensdag-markt
Spinolarei
Choco-Story
St-Jansstr
St-Walburgastr
Philipstockstr
Crowne Plaza
Burg
Canal Cruises
View Canal
Eekhoutpoort
Dijver
Canal Cruises

Spanjaardstr
St-Jansplein
Mallebergplaats
Hoogstr
Burg
Wollestr
Gruthusestr

Frietmuseum
Kraanrei
Kraanplein
Vlamingstr
Eiermarkt
Markt
Hallestr
St-Niklaasstr
Nieuwstr
Mariastr

Augustijnenrei
Kortewinkel
Vlamingstr
Kuipersstr
Markt
St-Amandsstr
Simon Stevinplein
Oude Burg
Steenstr

St-Jorisstr
Rode Haanstr
Boterhuis
St-Jakobsstr
Muntplein
Geldmuntstr
Hallestr
Kopstr
Zilverstr

Miraelstraat
Grauwwerkersstr
Kopstr
Giststr

Ezelstr
Azijnstr
Pottenmakersstr
Oude Zak
St-Jakobs-plein
Geerwijnstr
Moerstr
Ontvangersstr
Helmstr
Noordzandstr
Naaldstr

Zakske
Leeuwstr
St-Jakobs-plein
Wulfhagestr
Dweersstr
Korte Vuldersstr

Sights

Jeruzalemkerk CHURCH

1 ◉ Map p32, D5

In western St-Anna is one of Bruges' oddest churches, the 15th-century structure built by the Adornes family. Supposedly based upon Jerusalem's Church of the Holy Sepulchre, it has a gruesome altarpiece covered in skull motifs and an effigy of Christ's corpse tucked away in the rear minichapel. The black-marble tomb of Anselm Adornes contains only his heart, presumably all that could be carried back to Bruges after he was murdered in Scotland in 1483. (Peperstraat 1; adult/child €2.50/1.50; ⏱10am-5pm Mon-Sat)

Canal View CANAL

2 ◉ Map p32, C7

Don't miss the superb canal view from outside 't Klein Venetie cafe. With the belfry towering above a perfect gaggle of medieval house-fronts, the view is lovely any time, but it's especially compelling at dusk as the floodlights come on. From here, canalside Dijver leads southwest towards Bruges' foremost city museums. (www.360cities.net/image/rozenhoedkaai-brugge)

OLV-ter-Potterie MUSEUM

3 ◉ Map p32, D2

Admission to this small historical church-hospital complex is free with a

Understand
Laced Up

There are two main ways of making lace (kant/dentelle in Dutch/French). Needlepoint lace (naaldkant) uses a single thread to embroider a pattern on a piece of cloth or paper that will eventually be discarded. Originally Italian, the technique was perfected in Brussels, and the classic needlepoint stitch is still known as 'corded Brussels'. In contrast, bobbin lace (kloskant) creates a web of interlinked threads using multiple threaded-bobbins meticulously twisted using a maze of hand-placed pins. It's an astonishingly fiddly process, believed to have originated in 14th-century Bruges. Some of the finest known handmade samples, made using hundreds of bobbins, originated in Binche, while Chantilly, an originally French subform using black cotton, was for years a noted speciality craft of Geraardsbergen. To save time and avoid errors, 19th-century Brussels manufacturers came up with cut-thread lace in which a series of smaller bobbin-lace details are sewn together to create larger pieces. The most typical styles were Rosaline, where little rose details were often pearl-embroidered, and Duchesse, with flower-and-leaf motifs. These days much lace-making is mechanised, but the handmade craft can still be seen at Bruges' Kantcentrum (map p32; D5; p31). Lace also makes a great Bruges souvenir (p31).

St-Janshospitaal museum ticket. Ring the bell to gain entry and you'll find fine 15th- to 16th-century art. The lushly baroque church section houses the reliquary of St-Idesbaldus and a polychrome wooden relief of Mary breastfeeding baby Jesus. In more prudish later centuries, the Virgin's nipple received a lacy camouflage, rendering the scene bizarrely impractical. (Potterierei 79; adult/concession €4/3; ⏱9.30am-12.30pm & 1.30-5pm)

Crowne Plaza Hotel   HISTORIC SITE

4 ⊙ Map p32, C6

In the 1990s, when excavating for the foundations of the Crowne Plaza Hotel, workers literally hit a wall. This wall, it turned out, belonged to the 10th-century St-Donaas church (where Charles the Good, Count of Flanders is believed to have been assassinated in 1127), which later became a cathedral. Construction was allowed to proceed, provided that the remains were accessible to the public at no cost. It's occasionally closed for hotel conferences, but otherwise you're free to go down at any time (within reason) to find old maps, paintings, tombs and respite from the crowds above ground. (Burg 10)

Choco-Story   MUSEUM

5 ⊙ Map p32, C6

A highly absorbing chocolate museum tracing the cocoa bean back to its role as an Aztec currency. Learn about choco-history, watch a video on cocoa production and sample a praline that's

made as you watch (last demonstration 4.45pm). (www.choco-story.be; Wijnzakstraat 2, on Sint-Jansplein; adult/child €8/5, combined ticket with Diamantmuseum €14; ⏱10am-5pm)

Frietmuseum   MUSEUM

6 ⊙ Map p32, B6

Follows the history of the potato from ancient Inca gravesites to the Belgian fryer. The entry fee includes a discount token for the basement **frituur** (frituur fries €2; ⏱ 11am-3pm) that immodestly claims to fry the world's ultimate chips. (☎050 34 01 50; www.frietmuseum.be; Vlamingstraat 33; adult/child/concession €7/5/6; ⏱10am-5pm, closed Christmas–mid-Jan)

Eating

Pro Deo   BELGIAN €€

7 ✗ Map p32, E5

A snug and romantic restaurant in a 16th-century whitewashed gabled building. The owner couple bring a personal touch, and serve up superb Belgian dishes such as *stoofvlees* (traditional stew). (☎050 33 73 55; www.bistroprodeo.be; Langestraat 161; mains €19-28; ⏱11.45am-1.45pm & 6-9.30pm Tue-Fri, 6-10pm Sat)

De Stove   INTERNATIONAL €€

8 ✗ Map p32, B7

Just 20 seats keep this gem intimate. Fish caught daily is the house speciality, but the monthly changing menu also includes the likes of wild boar fillet on oyster mushrooms. Everything, from the bread to the ice cream, is homemade. Despite perennially rave reviews, this calm, one-room, family restaurant remains friendly, reliable and inventive, without a hint of tourist tweeness. (☑050 33 78 35; www.restaurant-destove.be; Kleine St-Amandsstraat 4; mains €19-34, menu without/with wine €49/67; ☺noon-1.30pm Sat & Sun, 7-9pm Fri-Tue)

Den Gouden Karpel SEAFOOD €

9 ✖ Map p32, C7

Takeaway or eat in, this sleek little *café*-bar is a great location for a jump-ingly fresh seafood lunch, right by the fish market. Crab sandwiches, smoked salmon salads, shrimp croquettes and oysters are on the menu. (☑050 33 33 89; www.dengoudenkarpel.be; Vismarkt 9-11; mains from €4; ☺11am-6pm Tue-Sat)

De Bottelier MEDITERRANEAN €€

10 ✖ Map p32, A6

Decorated with hats and old clocks, this adorable little restaurant sits above a wine shop overlooking a delightful handkerchief of canalside garden. Pasta/veg dishes cost from €9/13.50. Diners are predominantly local. Reservations are wise. (☑050 33 18 60; www.debottelier.com; St-Jakobsstraat 63; mains from €16; ☺noon-10pm Tue-Fri, 7-10pm Sat)

De Karmeliet INTERNATIONAL €€€

11 ✖ Map p32, D6

Chef Geert Van Hecke's intricate combinations, such as stuffed courgette with poached quail eggs, caviar, king crab and mousseline champagne, have earned him a trio of Michelin stars. The setting is slightly austere, but gourmands will be too busy swooning to notice. Lunch is slightly easier on your wallet. Book well ahead, especially for weekends. (☑050 33 82 59; www.dekarmeliet.be; Langestraat 19; mains from €70, menus from €85; ☺noon-1.30pm & 7-9.30pm Tue-Sat; ✱)

Chagall BELGIAN €€

12 ✖ Map p32, A7

Checked olive banquettes, candles, shelves cluttered with knick-knacks

○ Local Life
Late-Night Eating

If your stomach demands more than just chips or kebabs after 11pm, try the effortlessly elegant, open-kitchened restaurant Christophe (p57), which serves until 1am. Or, before 3am, you could tuck into typical Flemish fare at the cosily historic **'t Gulden Vlies** (☑050 33 47 09; www.tguldenvlies.be; Mallebergplaats 17; mains €14.50-25; ☺7pm-3am Wed-Sun). Most restaurants lining the Markt offer breakfasts with a view from €7, but check carefully what's included before sitting down. If you just want coffee and a croissant, the cheapest deal is at chain bakery **Panos** (Zuidzandstraat 29; coffee/croissant €1.80/1.10; ☺7am-6.30pm Mon-Sat, 11am-6.30pm Sun).

Understand
Belgian Chocolate

Chocolate is fundamentally a mix of cocoa paste, sugar and cocoa butter in varying proportions. Dark chocolate uses the most cocoa paste, milk chocolate mixes in milk powder, and white chocolate uses cocoa butter but no cocoa paste at all. Mouth-watering Belgian chocolate is arguably the world's best because it sticks religiously to these pure ingredients, while other countries allow cheaper vegetable fats to replace some of the cocoa butter.

The essential Belgian chocs are pralines and creamy manons – filled bite-sized chocolates sold from an astonishing range of specialist shops. Here glove-clad assistants wrap whatever you select from the enchanting display – it's fine to buy just a single chocolate. Price varies radically according to the brand. It's hard to go wrong with ubiquitous chain Leonidas, though many locals prefer pricier Neuhaus, Corné or Galler. Stylish black-box presentation, specialist bean sources and innovative flavours make Pierre Marcolini the brand of choice for the wealthy and fashion conscious. A 'boutique' chocolatier with a special reputation is Chocolate Line, which created its nasally injested choco-shot for the Rolling Stones.

and an upright piano make you feel like you're dining in a family home. Seafood, such as several variations on eel, is Chagall's forte, but it also does daily meat specials and good deals on two- and three-course menus. (☑050 33 61 12; www.restaurantchagall.be; St-Amandsstraat 40; mains €10-22; ⊙closed Wed)

Gran Kaffee De Passage
BISTRO €

14 ✗ Map p32, A8

A mix of regulars and travellers staying at the adjoining hostel, Passage, give this candlelit, alternative art deco–styled bistro one of the best atmospheres in town. Its menu of hearty traditional dishes, such as *stoverij* (local meat in beer sauce),

as well as filling tofu creations, is a bargain. (☑050 34 02 32; www.passagebruges.com; Dweersstraat 26-28; mains €10-16.50; ⊙5-11pm Tue-Thu & Sun, noon-11pm Fri & Sat)

Da Vinci
ICE CREAM €

14 ✗ Map p32, A7

Not being able to choose between the 40 luscious flavours of freshly made ice cream at this *gelateria* (gelato shop) is a good thing, as it means you'll be offered small spoonfuls of free samples to help you decide (of course, that might just make the decision harder). Scoops cost just €1.30; in high summer it stays open until 11pm. (☑050 33 36 50; Geldmuntstraat 34; scoop €1.30; ⊙closed mid-Nov–Feb)

Tous Paris

SANDWICHES €

15 ✖ Map p32, A8

If you and your arteries need a break from waffles and fries, this gourmet grocer offers a welcome alternative by way of fresh salads, quiches and made-to-order sandwiches on white or wholegrain baguettes. (📞050 33 79 02; Zuidzandstraat 31; snacks €3-8; ⏱closed Wed & Thu)

In 't Nieuwe Museum

PUB €€

16 ✖ Map p32, E7

So called because of the museum-like collection of brewery plaques, money boxes and other mementos of *café* life adorning the walls, this family-owned local favourite serves five kinds of *dagschotel* (dish of the day) for lunch (€7 to €12.50), and succulent meat cooked on a 17th-century open fire in the evenings. (📞050 33 12 22; Hooistraat

Local Life
Mixing with the Locals

Set around a courtyard comprising characterful brick buildings, **De Republiek** (www.derepubliek.be; St-Jakobsstraat 36; ⏱11am-late), a big buzzing space, is super-popular with Bruggelingen (Bruges locals). DJs hit the decks on Friday and Saturday nights and there's a range of well-priced meals, including vegetarian options, available until midnight, plus a long cocktail list.

42; mains €16-22; ⏱noon-2pm & 6-10pm Thu-Tue, closed lunch Sat)

Ryad

INDIAN, MOROCCAN €€

17 ✖ Map p32, C6

Indian curries supplement the usual couscous and tagines offered by this atmospheric Moroccan restaurant that's heavily perfumed with incense. Upstairs is a cosy cushioned 'Berber' tea lounge. (📞050 33 13 55; Hoogstraat 32; mains €18-24, lunch menu €10.50; ⏱noon-2.30pm & 6-10.30pm Thu-Mon)

Est Wijnbar

TAPAS €

This attractive little wine bar near the canal (see 2 ⊙ Map p32, C7) is a pleasantly informal supper spot, with *raclette*, pasta, snacks and salads on the menu, and tasty desserts. It's especially lively on Sunday nights, when you can catch live jazz, blues and occasionally other musical styles from 8.30pm. The building dates back to 1637. (📞050 33 38 39; www.wijnbarest.be; Braambergstraat 7; mains €10-14, tapas €4-10; ⏱4pm-midnight Fri-Mon; 🎵)

Sans Cravate

FRENCH €€€

18 ✖ Map p32, E5

Bare brick walls, a modernistic fireplace and striking contemporary modern ceramics form a stage for this open-kitchened 'cooking theatre' that prides itself on its gastronomic French cuisine and fresh ingredients. (📞050 67 83 10; www.sanscravate.be; Langestraat 159; mains €38-42, menus €58-89; ⏱noon-2pm Tue-Fri, 7-9.30pm Tue-Sat)

View of the Belfort and canals (p34)

Drinking

't Poatersgat
PUB

19 Map p32, B5

Look carefully for the concealed hole in the wall and follow the staircase down into this cross-vaulted cellar glowing with ethereal white lights and flickering candles. 't Poatersgat (which means 'the Monk's Hole' in the local dialect) has 120 Belgian beers on the menu, including a smashing selection of Trappists. (www.poatersgat.com; Vlaamingstraat 82; ⊙5pm-late)

Herberg Vlissinghe
PUB

20 Map p32, D5

Luminaries have frequented Bruges' oldest pub for 500 years; local legend has it that Rubens once painted an imitation coin on the table here and then did a runner. The interior is gorgeously preserved with wood panelling and a wood-burning stove, but in summer the best seats are in the shady garden where you can play boule. (☏050 34 37 37; www.cafevlissinghe. be; Blekerstraat 2; ⊙11am-10pm Wed & Thu, to midnight Fri & Sat, to 7pm Sun)

Understand

Bruges Matins

The precocious wealth and independence of Bruges' medieval guildsmen brought political tensions with their French overlords. In 1302, when guildsmen refused to pay a new round of taxes, the French sent in a 2000-strong army to garrison the town. Uncowed, Pieter De Coninck, Dean of the Guild of Weavers, and Jan Breydel, Dean of the Guild of Butchers, led a revolt that would go down in Flanders' history books as the 'Bruges Matins' (Brugse Metten). Early in the morning on 18 May, guildsmen crept into town and murdered anyone who could not correctly pronounce the hard-to-say Dutch phrase *'schild en vriend'* (shield and friend). This revolt sparked a widespread Flemish rebellion. A short-term Flemish victory six weeks later at the Battle of the Golden Spurs near Kortrijk gave medieval Flanders a very short-lived moment of independence.

De Garre

PUB

21 Map p32, B7

Try its very own and fabulous Garre draught beer, which comes with a thick floral head in a glass that's almost a brandy balloon; staff will only serve you three of these due to the head-spinning 11% alcohol percentage. The hidden two-floor *estaminet* (tavern) also stocks dozens of other fine Belgian brews, including remarkable Struise Pannepot (€3.50). (☑050 34 10 29; www.degarre.be; Garre 1; ⊗noon-midnight Mon-Thu, to 1am Fri & Sat)

Cambrinus

PUB

22 Map p32, C6

Hundreds of varieties of beer are available at this 17th-century sculpture-adorned brasserie-pub, as well as traditional Belgian- and Italian-inspired snacks and meals. (☑050 33 23 28; www.cambrinus.eu; Philipstockstraat 19; ⊗11am-11pm Sun-Thu, to late Fri & Sat)

Rose Red

BAR

23 Map p32, C6

Outstanding beers from 50 of the best breweries in Belgium, served by charming and informative staff in this pink-hued and rose-scattered bar. It keeps five to six beers on tap and 150 bottles, or you can taste four beers for €10. Snack on tapas-style dishes, including cheese produced by the Trappist monks of Chimay (from €3.50). (☑050 33 90 51; www.cordoeanier. be/en/rosered.php; Cordoeaniersstraat 16; ⊗11am-11pm Tue-Sun)

Opus Latino

PUB

24 Map p32, C7

Modernist *café* with weather-worn terrace tables right at the waterside – where a canal dead-ends beside a Buddha-head fountain. Access is via the easily missed shopping passage that links Wollestraat to Burg, emerging near the Heilig-Bloedpro-cessie. Serves tapas, as well as more substantial snacks. (📞050 33 97 46; Burg 15; beer/snacks/tapas from €2.20/8.50/6; ⊙11am-11pm Thu-Tue)

Merveilleux Tearoom

CAFE

25 🍴 Map p32, A7

Elegant marble-floored tearoom on a cobbled passage near the Markt. Coffee comes with a dainty homemade biscuit and sometimes a little glass of strawberry ice cream or chocolate mousse. Pretty cakes and tea are on offer too. (📞050 61 02 09; www.merveil-leux.eu; Muntpoort 8; high tea €11, mains €15-24; ⊙10am-6pm)

Entertainment

Retsin's Lucifernum

CLUB

26 ⭐ Map p32, C6

A former Masonic lodge owned by a self-proclaimed vampire: ring the bell on a Sunday night, pass the voodoo temple and hope you're invited inside where an otherworldly candle-lit bar may be serving potent rum cocktails and serenading you with live Latin music. Or maybe not. It's always a surprise. Don't miss the graves in the tropical garden. (📞0476 35 06 51; www.lucifernum.be; Twijnstraat 6-8; admission incl drink €10; ⊙8-11pm Sun)

Cinema Lumière

CINEMA

27 ⭐ Map p32, A6

Just a couple of blocks back from the Markt, this art-house cinema screens a well-chosen program of foreign films in their original languages and is home to the **Cinema Novo Film Festival**. (📞050 34 34 65; www.lumiere.be; St-Jakobsstraat 36)

Koninklijke Stadsschouwburg

THEATRE

28 ⭐ Map p32, B6

Cultuurcentrum Brugge coordinates theatrical and concert events at several venues, including this majestic 1869 theatre. Opera, classical concerts, theatre and dance are on offer; out front is a statue of Papageno, from Mozart's *The Magic Flute*. (📞050 44 30 60; Vlamingstraat 29)

☑️ Top Tip

Bargain Bruges

If you're visiting more than a couple of sights, invest in a Bruges City Card (p159), which gives free entry to all the main city museums, plus various attractions including private ventures such as Choco-Story and De Halve Maan brewery. You'll also score a canal-boat ride (which shouldn't be missed, however cheesy it may seem), as well as discounts on bicycle rental, concerts, films and theatre.

Du Phare

LIVE MUSIC

29 ⭐ Map p32, D1

Tucked into the remains of one of Bruges' original town gates, this off-the-beaten-track tavern serves up huge portions of couscous (and offers free bread, a rarity in Belgium). But Du Phare is best known for its live blues and jazz sessions – check the website for dates. Bus 4 stops out the front. (📞050 34 35 90; www.duphare.be; Sasplein 2; ⏰kitchen 11.30am-3pm & 6pm-midnight, bar 11.30am-late, closed Tue)

Entrenous

CLUB

30 ⭐ Map p32, E5

A real nightclub in the centre of the city. A very youthful crowd packs out the DJ nights, gigs and after parties. (📞050 34 10 93; www.bauhauszaal.be; Langestraat 145; ⏰10pm-late Fri & Sat)

Joey's Café

LIVE MUSIC

31 ⭐ Map p32, A8

These days Joey's is run by Stevie, who performs with local band Cajun Moon and consequently, this dark, intimate bar is a gathering spot for Bruges' musos. You can sometimes catch live music here (call to check dates), or chill out with a creamy Stevie cocktail or Joey's Tripel any time. (📞050 34 12 64; Zuidzandstraat 16a; ⏰11.30am-late Mon-Sat)

Vinkenzettingen

LIVE PERFORMANCE

32 ⭐ Map p32, E4

There's no set schedule, but one place you might witness the eccentric (if hardly exciting) 'traditional sport' of finch singing is along Hugo Verrieststraat, early on summer Sunday mornings. Dating from the late 16th century, the idea is to find which caged chaffinch, within a wooden box, can chirrup more times in an hour than its competitor.

Only a specific 'susk-*weet*' sound is acceptable, with some potty *vinkeniers* (finch fanciers) claiming that birds from Wallonia can't pronounce correct Dutch! (www.avibo.be; Hugo Verrieststraat)

Shopping

Vismarkt

MARKET

33 🔒 Map p32, C7

At the colonnaded Vismarkt, fishmongers have been selling their North Sea produce for centuries. These days only a few vendors set up on the cold stone slabs, but it's still worth a wander. Join locals buying snacks such as *maatjes* (herring fillets). On weekends, the Vismarkt and nearby Dijver are taken over by antique and bric-a-brac stalls. (Steenhouwersdijk; ⏰8am-1pm Tue-Sat)

De Reyghere Reisboekhandel

BOOKS

34 🔒 Map p32, B7

Well-stocked travel bookshop. (📞050 33 34 03; www.reisboekhandel.be; Markt 13; ⏰9.30am-noon Tue-Sat & 2-6pm Mon-Sat)

De Biertempel

FOOD & DRINK

35 🔒 Map p32, B6

Beer specialist shop where you can even pick up a well-priced bottle of Westvleteren. (☎050 34 37 30; Philipstockstraat 7; ⊙10am-6pm)

Rombaux

MUSIC

36 🔒 Map p32, C6

Here since 1920, this large, family-run music shop specialises in classical music, jazz, world music, folk and Flemish music, and is the kind of place where you can browse for hours. It also sells sheet music and accoustic guitars. (☎050 33 25 75; www.rombaux.be; Mallebergplaats 13; ⊙2-6.30pm Mon, 10am-12.30pm & 2-6.30pm Tue-Fri, 10am-6pm Sat)

Olivier Strelli

FASHION

37 🔒 Map p32, A8

Belgium's best-known designer, who has an emphasis on colourful scarves, shoes and watches. (☎050 34 38 37; strelli.be; Zuidzandstraat 11/13; ⊙10am-6pm Mon-Sat)

2-Be

FOOD & DRINK

38 🔒 Map p32, C7

Vast range of Belgian products from beers to biscuits in a snazzy, central location, but prices can be exorbitant. Its 'beer wall' is worth a look, as is the wonderfully located canalside bar terrace, where 'monster' 3L draught beers (€19.50) are surely Belgium's biggest. (www.2-be.biz; Wollestraat 53; ⊙10am-7pm)

Explore

Groeningemuseum & the South

Bruges may strike visitors as somewhat like an open-air museum, particularly in this area where the historic buildings, galleries and churches cluster. True, Bruges' harmonious Gothic architecture, willow-lined waterways and market-filled squares are almost impossibly quaint. But beyond the souvenir shops you'll find cosy backstreet bars and *cafés* (pubs), young artisans and a palpable sense of history.

The Sights in a Day

☼ Start by immersing yourself in art, first at the **Groeninge-museum** (p46) for an overview of Belgian art history, then at the **Memlingmuseum** (p48), a wonderful and historic showcase for six master-works by Hans Memling. Your museum ticket also allows you to see the ancient hospital building in which the museum is situated, in addition to an interesting 17th-century pharmacy.

☼ Break for lunch at **Den Dijver** (p56), where food is cooked in the country's finest beer. Here you're well placed to make a postprandial and leisurely **boat cruise** (p53): seeing the city from a canal is an essential Bruges experience. Wander down to the **begijnhof** (p50), whose courtyard is an oasis of calm, and visit the austerely beautiful house museum there. In good weather stroll to the Minnewater Park and relax among the flowerbeds.

☾ For a pleasant and laidback sup-per on a quiet back street try **De Stoepa** (p56), where decent bistro food is served. After dinner, take a stroll around this residential area for a taste of 'real' Bruges. Finish with a classical concert at the **Concertgebouw** (p58), Bruges' concession to modernity.

◉ Top Sights

Groeningemuseum (p46)

Memlingmuseum (p48)

Begijnhof (p50)

♥ Best of Bruges

Best for the Flemish Primitives
Groeningemuseum (p46)

Memlingmuseum (p48)

Best Museums
't Begijnhuisje (p51)

Diamantmuseum (p55)

Best Green Spaces
Minnewater (p56)

Begijnhof (p50)

Getting There

🚆 **Train** From the train station it takes around 20 minutes to walk to the centre of Bruges.

🚌 **Bus** Any bus marked 'Centrum' runs to the Markt, from where it's a short stroll south to the Groeningemuseum.

Top Sights
Groeningemuseum

This is a candidate for Bruges' most celebrated art gallery. While not enormous, it packs in an astonishingly rich collection of Flemish Primitive and Renaissance works. There are some intriguing early images of the city of Bruges itself, as well as an eye-popping Hieronymous Bosch. More meditative works include Jan Van Eyck's radiant *Madonna with Canon George Van der Paele* (1436) and Hans Memling's *Moreel Triptych* (1484). Later artists also get a look in, including superstar symbolist Fernand Khnopff; plus it has a canvas each from Magritte and Delvaux.

◉ Map p52, D2

www.brugge.be

Dijver 12

adult/concession €8/6

⊙ 9.30am-5pm Tue-Sun

Madonna with Canon George van der Paele, by Jan Van Eyck

Don't Miss

City as Patron
The gallery gets underway with absorbing images of the city commissioned by its merchant patrons. A map – more like an aerial view – shows 15th-century Bruges in every detail, from spinning windmills to tall ships in the harbour. Gerard David's grisly *Judgement of Cambyses* (1498) also features the cityscape.

Flemish Primitives
Things take off artistically in the Flemish Primitives room, crammed with works by Jan Van Eyck, Roger Van der Weyden, Hans Memling and Gerard David. These pieces depict the conspicuous wealth of the city with glitteringly realistic artistry. Typical is the *Madonna by the Master of the Embroidered Foliage,* where the rich fabric of the Madonna's robe meets the 'real' foliage at her feet with exquisite detail. Jan Van Eyck's wonderful portraits also reflect these traits, as well as adding a dimension of psychological realism.

Townscapes & Landscapes
Visions of the city surface again in this room, with picturesque scenes by Jan Anton Garemijn, as well as Auguste Van de Steene's austere view of the market square.

Flemish Expressionism
These works from the 1920s show the influence of Cubism and German Expressionism on Flemish artists – most striking are Constant Permeke's earth-coloured depictions of peasant life in *Pap Eaters* and *The Angelus*. Two further rooms also cover the modern period, ending with works from the '60s and '70s, which show the influence of arch-surrealist Magritte.

☑ Top Tips

▶ As with most Belgian attractions, the museum is closed on Monday.

▶ You can visit for free with the Bruges City Card (p159).

▶ The museum is justifiably popular, so arrive as early as possible at busy times of year.

▶ If you're short on time, focus on works by the Flemish Primitives, which are the high-point of the museum.

▶ Dazzle other gallery goers with your knowledge: you'll notice the work of the 'primitives' is pretty sophisticated – the name derives from the Latin *primus* (first), as the artists were the first to adopt new painting techniques.

✕ Take a Break

A short walk along the canal from the museum brings you to stylish Den Dyjver (p56), serving top-quality Belgian cuisine.

Top Sights
Memlingmuseum

In the restored chapel of a 12th-century hospital building with superb timber beamwork, St-Janshospitaal shows various historical medical implements and medically themed paintings, but is best known for the Memlingmuseum, which exhibits six glowing masterpieces by 15th-century artist Hans Memling, including the enchanting *Reliquary of St Ursula*. Memling was born in Frankfurt, but spent most of his painting career in Bruges. Your ticket also covers a visit to the hospital's restored 17th-century *apotheek* (pharmacy), located in the same complex of buildings.

◉ Map p52, C3

Mariastraat 38

adult/child/concession €8/free/6

⊙ 9.30am-5pm Tue-Sun

St-Janshospitaal

Don't Miss

The Memling Paintings
The old hospital chapel is dedicated to a small but priceless collection of works by Hans Memling, which glow in the dim light. Largest is the triptych of St John the Baptist and St John the Evangelist, commissioned by the hospital church as an altarpiece. Look out for St Catherine (with spinning wheel) and St Barbara, both seated at the feet of the Virgin. Memling's secular portrayals are just as engrossing, such as the delicate *Portrait of a Young Woman* (1480), where the subject's hands rest on the painted frame of her portrait.

The Reliquary of St Ursula
This gilded oak reliquary looks like a mini Gothic cathedral, painted by Memling with scenes from the life of St Ursula, including highly realistic Cologne cityscapes. The devout Ursula was a Breton princess betrothed to a pagan prince. She agreed to marry him on the condition she could make a pilgrimage to Rome (via Cologne) with 11,000 virgins. All were murdered on the return journey by the king of the Huns, along with Ursula and her betrothed.

St-Janshospitaal Artefacts
Lofty St-Janshospitaal has been elegantly restored to show off both the exposed beams of the 12th-century building and an array of artefacts relating to the museum. The latter include tortuous-looking medical implements, hospital sedan chairs and a gruesome 1679 painting of an anatomy class.

☑ Top Tips

▶ Buy a Bruges City Card (p159) if you're seeing a number of museums in the city – it also offers discounts on travel, tickets and some restaurants.

▶ The museum shop has an excellent in-depth guide to the exhibits and paintings (€12.50).

▶ Though it's not the main event, the 17th-century *apotheek* is worth a look. The glazed cloisters of the building you walk through to enter it are very attractive, and the pharmacy itself is a beautiful tiled space with rows of jars and a pendulum clock.

▶ Take a peek into the Trustees Room, adjoining the pharmacy. It's lined with portraits of bewigged and beruffed trustees.

✕ Take a Break

Head down Mariastraat till it turns into Katelijnestraat, to enjoy the vegie offerings of De Bron (p56).

Top Sights
Begijnhof

Bruges' delightful *begijnhof* dates from the 13th century. Although the last *begijn* has long since passed away, today residents of the pretty, whitewashed garden complex include a convent of Benedictine nuns. Despite the hoards of summer tourists, the *begijnhof* remains a remarkably tranquil haven, and in spring a carpet of daffodils adds to the quaintness of the scene. Just inside the main entrance, 't Begijnhuisje is a typical *begijnhof* house now converted into an endearing four-room museum.

Map p52, B4

Wijngaardstraat

admission free

6.30am-6.30pm

Beguinage church

Don't Miss

't Begijnhuisje

This charming 17th-century house is now a domestic **museum** (adult/child/senior €2/1/1.50; ⏰10am-5pm Mon-Sat, 2.30-5pm Sun). In the rustic kitchen with its blue and white Delft tiles you'll see a Louvain stove that extends into the room from the hearth so that people can sit round it. The sitting room displays black Chantilly lace (p34), while the austere bedroom has a portrait showing a traditional *begijn* costume. The dining room features a simple wooden cupboard, which served as a pantry, china store and pull-out dining table; beyond the house is a simple stone cloister with a well.

Church of the Beguinage

The baroque church features a flamboyant high altar, 17th-century choir stalls, and chubby putti adorning the choir screen. Outside, tall elm trees frame the view of the whitewashed houses, and despite the occasional crowds there's still a secluded, village-like air to the place.

The Minnewater

Known in English as the 'Lake of Love', the Minnewater canal is adjacent to a charming park, which really does give this area a romantic quality. There are plenty of sheltered paths and benches to retreat to on a sunny day. In Bruges' medieval heyday, this is where ships from far and wide would unload their cargoes of wool, wine, spices and silks.

☑ Top Tips

▶ Outside the *begijn-hof*'s 1776 gateway bridge lies a tempting array of terraced restaurants and waffle peddlers: handy if you want a snack nearby, though prices are on the high side.

▶ Look out for the horse fountain over the bridge – the sculpted horse's heads spurt water, allowing carriage-drivers to fill buckets and give their horses a drink.

▶ The Minnewater is a good location for a picnic, so you might want to bring food with you.

▶ Photograph the *begijn-hof* at dawn or dusk for maximum tranquility and good light.

✕ Take a Break

Stroll down a tranquil backstreet to delightful De Stoepa (p56), for bistro food and a pleasant hippy vibe.

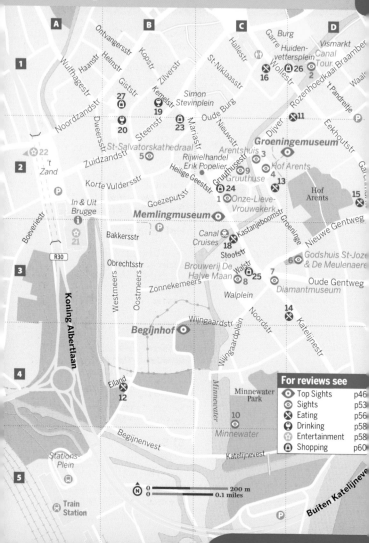

Sights

Onze-Lieve-Vrouwekerk   CHURCH

1 ⊙ Map p52, C2

This large, somewhat sober 13th-century church sports an enormous tower that's currently 'wrapped' for extensive renovation. Inside, it's best known for Michelangelo's serenely contemplative 1504 *Madonna and Child* statue, the only such work by Michelangelo to leave Italy during the artist's lifetime; look out also for the *Adoration of the Shepherds* by Pieter Pourbus.

In the church's apse, the treasury section displays some splendid 15th- and 16th-century artworks plus the fine stone-and-bronze tombs of Charles the Bold (Karel de Stoute) and his daughter, Mary of Burgundy, whose pivotal marriage dragged the Low Countries into the Hapsburg empire, with far-reaching consequences. (Church of Our Lady; Mariastraat; ⊙9.30am-4.50pm Mon-Sat, 1.30-4.50pm Sun)

Canal Tour   BOAT TOUR

2 ⊙ Map p52, D1

Taking a Canal Tour is a must. Yep, it's touristy, but what isn't in Bruges? Viewing the city from the water gives it a totally different feel than by foot. Cruise down Spiegelrei towards Jan Van Eyckplein and it's possible to imagine Venetian merchants entering the city centuries ago and meeting under the slender turret of the Poortersloge building up ahead. (adult/child €7.60/3.40; ⊙10am-6pm Mar–mid-Nov)

Arentshuis   GALLERY

3 ⊙ Map p52, C2

With your Groeningemuseum ticket, admission is free to this stately 18th-century patrician house displaying the powerful paintings and dark-hued etchings of Frank Brangwyn (1867–1956), a Bruges-born artist of Welsh parentage. His images of WWI – he was an official war artist – are particularly powerful. (Dijver 16; adult/child/concession €4/free/3; ⊙9.30am-5pm Tue-Sun)

Hof Arents   PARK

4 ⊙ Map p52, C2

Behind the Arentshuis, Hof Arents is a charming little park where a hump-backed pedestrian bridge, **St-Bonifaciusbrug**, crosses the canal for idyllic views. Generally nicknamed Lovers' Bridge, it's where many a Bruges citizen steals their first kiss. Privileged guests staying at the **Guesthouse Nuit Blanche** (☎0494 40 04 47; www.bb-nuitblanche.com; Groeninge 2; d €175-195) get the romantic moonlit scene all to themselves once the park has closed. (admission free; ⊙7am-10pm Apr-Sep, to 9pm Oct-Mar)

St-Salvatorskathedraal   CATHEDRAL

5 ⊙ Map p52, B2

Stacked subtowers top the massive central tower of 13th-century

Understand

Flemish Primitives

Belgium's celebrated art heritage blossomed in 15th-century Bruges with painters now known as the Flemish Primitives. It may seem an odd term given that not all were Flemish and their work was anything but primitive – the term actually derives from the Latin *primus,* meaning first, an indication of their innovative and experimental approach. They pioneered a technique of painting in oil on oak boards, adding thin layers of paint to produce jewel-bright colours and exquisite detail.

Their radiant use of colour and detailed depictions of secular subjects greatly influenced the course of European art. Especially notable was Jan Van Eyck (c 1390–1441), who became wealthy combining painting with a lucrative sinecure as royal valet to the powerful Dukes of Burgundy. Van Eyck lived in Bruges; the Groeningemuseum (p46) has some superb canvases by him, including an intimate portrait of his wife. Other major names include Rogier Van der Weyden (c 1400–94) and Dutchman Gerard David (c 1460–1523), both predominantly Bruges-based.

Another star of the period was Hans Memling (c 1440–1494). It's thought that he came to Bruges from Cologne aged around 25; already a fully trained artist, he may have trained for a period in Brussels under Rogier Van der Weyden. Memling swiftly became a favourite among the city's merchant patrons, and also began an association with St John's Hospital, which resulted in the commissioning of the glowing religious works now displayed in the Memlingmuseum (p48). Here you can also see his St Ursula reliquary, one of the city's most important treasures.

The Primitives' contemporary Hieronymous Bosch (c 1450–1516) worked mainly in the Netherlands, though the distinction between Dutch and Flemish painting is somewhat artificial, since before the late 16th century Belgium and the Netherlands were simply known as the Low Countries and artists frequently moved from one royal court or town to another. Bosch's most fascinating paintings are nightmarish visual parables filled with gruesome beasts and devilish creatures often devouring or torturing agonised humans. Bosch's work had obvious influences on the great 16th-century Flemish painter Pieter Brueghel the Elder. Works by both Bosch and Brueghel can be seen in the Groeningemuseum (p46).

St-Saviour's Cathedral. In daylight the construction looks somewhat dour, but once floodlit at night, it takes on a mesmerising fascination. The cathedral's interior is vastly high but feels oddly plain despite a selection of antique tapestries. Beneath the tower, a glass floor reveals some painted graves, and there's a passingly interesting **treasury** (Steenstraat; adult/child €2/1; ⏱2-5pm Sun-Fri) displaying 15th-century brasses and a 1559 triptych by Dirk Bouts. (Steenstraat; ⏱2-5.45pm Mon, 9am-noon & 2-5.45pm Tue-Fri, 9am-noon & 2-3.30pm Sat & Sun)

Godshuis St-Jozef & De Meulenaere
HISTORIC BUILDING

6 ⊙ Map p52, D3

One of the delights of wandering around Bruges is the chance of coming across a complex of *godshuizen* (almshouses). One of the town's cutest and most central *godshuizen* is Godshuis St Jozef & De Meulenaere. Enter through large black doors. (Nieuwe Gentweg 24)

Diamantmuseum
MUSEUM

7 ⊙ Map p52, C3

While Antwerp is now the centre of the diamond industry, the idea of polishing the stones with diamond 'dust' was originally pioneered in Bruges. This is the theme developed by this slick museum which also displays a lumpy, greenish 252-carat raw diamond and explains how the catchphrase 'Diamonds are Forever'

started as a De Beers marketing campaign. Diamond-polishing demonstrations (12.15pm and 3.15pm) cost €3 extra. (Diamond Museum; ☑050 34 20 56; www.diamondmuseum.be; Katelijnestraat 43; adult/senior & student €8/7, combined ticket with Choco-Story €14; ⏱10.30am-5.30pm)

Brouwerij De Halve Maan
BREWERY

8 ⊙ Map p52, C3

Founded in 1856, though there has been a brewery on the site since 1564, this is the last family *brouwerij* (brewhouse) in central Bruges. Multilingual 45-minute **guided visits** (tours €8; ⏱11am-4pm, to 5pm Sat) depart on the hour. They include a tasting but can sometimes be rather crowded. Alternatively, you can simply sip one of its excellent Brugse Zot (Bruges Fool, 7%) or Straffe Hendrik (Strong Henry, 9%) beers in the appealing brewery *café* (pub). (☑050 33 26 97; www.halvemaan.be; Walplein 26; ⏱10.30am-6pm, closed mid-Jan)

Gruuthuse
MUSEUM

9 ⊙ Map p52, C2

The museum takes its name from the flower and herb mixture *(gruut)* that used to flavour beer before the cultivation of hops. The romantic heraldic entrance in a courtyard of ivy-covered walls and dreaming spires is arguably more interesting than the rambling, somewhat unsatisfying decorative-arts exhibits within. The unusual view from the upstairs oratory window into the treasury-apse of the Onze-Lieve-Vrouwekerk is worth a look. (Dijver 17; adult/concession €8/6; ⏱9.30am-5pm Tue-Sun)

Minnewater
CANAL

10 ⊙ Map p52, C4

Known in English as the Lake of Love, the Minnewater harks back to Bruges' medieval heyday. This waterway was a dock from where ships as far afield as Russia came laden with cargoes of wool, wine, spices and silks and left loaded with Flemish cloth.

Eating

Den Dyjver
BELGIAN €€

11 🍴 Map p52, D1

Den Dyjver is a pioneer of fine beer cuisine where you match the brew you drink with the one the chef used to create the sauce on your plate. But this is no pub: beers come in wine glasses served on starched table cloths in an atmosphere of Burgundian grandeur. The lunch menu includes *amuse-bouche*, nibbles and coffee. (☑050 33 60 69; www.dyver.be; Dijver 5; mains €17-32, tasting menu €49; ⏱noon-2pm & 6.30-9.30pm Fri-Mon)

De Stoepa
BISTRO €€

12 🍴 Map p52, B4

A gem of a place in a peaceful residential setting with a slightly hippy/Buddhist feel. Oriental statues, terracotta-coloured walls, a metal stove and wooden floors and furniture give a homey but stylish feel. Best of all though is the leafy terrace garden. Tuck into the upmarket bistro-style food. (☑050 33 04 54; www.stoepa.be; Oostmeers 124; ⏱noon-2pm & 6pm-midnight Tue-Sat, noon-3pm & 6-11pm Sun)

Den Gouden Harynck
INTERNATIONAL €€€

13 🍴 Map p52, C2

Behind an ivy-clad facade, this uncluttered Michelin-starred restaurant garners consistent praise and won't hurt the purse quite as severely as certain better-known competitors. A lovely location: both central and secluded; exquisite dishes might include noisettes of venison topped with lardo and quince puree or seed-crusted fillet of bream. (☑050 33 76 37; www.dengoudenharynck.be; Groeninge 25; mains €38-46, set lunch menu €45, midweek dinner €60, surprise menu €89; ⏱noon-1.30pm & 7-9pm Tue-Fri, 7-9pm Sat)

De Bron
VEGETARIAN €

14 🍴 Map p52, D3

By the time this glass-roofed restaurant's doors open, a queue has usually formed outside, full of diners keen to get vegetarian fare direct from *de bron* (the source). Dishes are available in small, medium and large, and there are some delicious soups, such as pumpkin. Vegans are catered for on request. (☑050 33 45 26; Katelijnestraat 82; snacks from €5; ⏱11.45am-2pm Mon-Fri; 🍴)

Minnewater

Christophe
BELGIAN €€

15 Map p52, D2

A cool late-night bistro with marble table-tops and a decent range of Flemish staples such as fresh Zeebrugge shrimps. Excellent late-nighter. (☎050 344 892; www.christophe-brugge.be; Garenmarkt 34; mains €17-30; ☺6pm-1am Thu-Mon)

Bistro Arthies
BISTRO €€

16 Map p52, C1

Managed by Arthies, an interior designer who looks like a dashingly Gothic Billy Connolly. He uses a projected clock, giant black flower bowls and stylishly whacky lamps to create an ambience that's eccentric yet fashion-conscious. There's an all-day,€18 three-course menu. (☎050 33 43 13; www.arthies.com; Wollestraat 10; mains & mussels from €17; ☺noon-10pm Wed-Mon)

't Ganzespel
BELGIAN €

17 Map p54 D1

Providing a truly intimate eating experience in a lovely old gabled building, the owner serves classic Belgian dishes such as meatballs and *kalfsblanket* (veal in a creamy sauce), as well as pasta dishes. Upstairs are three idiosyncratic B&B guest rooms (double €55 to €85), one with a musical shower. (☎050 33 12 33; www.ganzespel.be; Ganzenstraat 37; mains from €9.50; ☺6-10pm Fri-Sun)

Local Life

Vintage

For something a bit different, have a drink at the **Vintage** (Map p52, B2; ☎050 34 30 63; www.thevintage.be; Westmeers 13; 11am-1am Mon, Tue & Thu, to 2am Fri & Sat, noon-1am Sun). Unusually hip for Bruges, it has a chilled out '60s/'70s vibe, and a vintage Vespa hanging from the roof. The sunny terrace is a nice spot for a Jupiler. Be warned: the theme parties can be quite raucous.

De Proeverie   CAFE €

18   Map p52, C3

A chintzy but appealing tearoom serving a variety of teas, gloopy hot chocolate, milkshakes and indulgent homemade sweets including crème brûlée, chocolate mousse and *merveilleux* (meringue, cream and chocolate) cake. Coffee comes with generous goodies on the side. (☎050 33 08 87; www.deproeverie.be; Katelijnstraat 5-6; snacks from €5; ☺9.30am-6pm)

Drinking

't Brugs Beertje   PUB

19   Map p54, B1

Legendary throughout Bruges, Belgium and beyond for its hundreds of Belgian brews, this cosy *bruin café* (brown cafe; traditional pub) is filled with old advertising posters and locals who are part of the furniture. It's one of those perfect

beer-bars with smoke-yellowed walls, enamel signs, hop-sprig ceilings and knowledgeable staff to help you choose from a book full of brews. (www.brugsbeertje.be; Kemelstraat 5; ☺4pm-midnight Mon, Thu & Sun, to 1am Fri & Sat)

Cafédraal   BAR

20   Map p54, B2

Attached to an upmarket seafood restaurant (mains €25 to €48), this remarkable cocktail bar is enclosed by beech hedges and red-brick-gabled buildings, and displays bottles in gilt 'holy' niches. Suavely classy. (☎050 34 08 45; www.cafedraal.be; Zilverstraat 38; beer/wine/cocktails from €2.80/5/10; ☺6pm-1am Tue-Thu, to 3am Fri & Sat)

Entertainment

Concertgebouw   CONCERT HALL

21   Map p52, A3

Bruges' stunning 21st-century concert hall is the work of architects Paul Robbrecht and Hilde Daem and takes its design cues from the city's three famous towers and red bricks. Theatre, classical music and dance are regularly staged. The tourist office is situated at street level. (☎050 47 69 99; www.concertgebouw.be; 't Zand 34; tickets from €10)

Cactus Muziekcentrum   LIVE MUSIC

22   Map p52, A2

Though small, this is the city's top venue for contemporary and world

Understand
Begijnhoven & Godshuizen

In the 12th century, large numbers of men from the Low Countries embarked on Crusades to the Holy Land and never returned. Their unchaperoned women-folk often felt obliged to seek security by joining a religious order. However, joining a convent required giving up one's worldly possessions and even one's name. A middle way, especially appealing to relatively wealthy widows, was to become a *begijn* (*béguine* in French). These lay sisters made Catholic vows including obedience and chastity, but could maintain their private wealth. They lived in a self-contained *begijnhof* (*béguinage* in French): a cluster of houses built around a central garden and church, surrounded by a protective wall. Land (normally at the outskirts of town) was typically granted by a pious feudal lord, but once established these all-female communities were self-sufficient. Most had a farm and vegetable garden and made supplementary income from lace-making and from benefactors who would pay the *begijnen* to pray for them.

In the 16th century, Holland's growing Protestantism meant that most Dutch *begijnhoven* were swept away. But Spanish-ruled Flanders was gripped by a fervently Catholic Counter-Reformation that reshaped the *begijn* movement. Rebuilt *begijnhoven* became hospice-style institutions with vastly improved funding. From 1583 the Archbishop of Mechelen decreed a standardised rulebook and a nunlike 'uniform' for *begijnen*, who at one point comprised almost 5% of Flanders' female population.

A century ago some 1500 *begijnen* remained in Belgium, but now only one remains, Marcella Pattyn in Kortrijk. Kortrijk's is one of 14 Flanders *begijnhoven* on the Unesco World Heritage List. Each is beautifully preserved albeit these days lived in by ordinary townsfolk, with Bruges' being one of the most idyllic.

Looking somewhat similar to *begijnhoven* but usually on a smaller scale are *godshuizen* (almshouses), typically featuring redbrick or whitewashed-shuttered cottages set around a tiny enclosed garden. Originally built by merchant guilds for their members or by rich sponsors to provide shelter for the poor (and to save the sponsors' souls), these days they're great places to peacefully unwind if you dare to push open their usually closed doors. Bruges has a remarkable 46 *godshuizen*.

music, live bands and international DJs. It also organises festivals including July's **Cactus Music Festival** (www.cactusfestival.be), held in the Minnewater park at the southern edge of the old city. (☎050 33 20 14; www.cactusmusic.be; Magdalenastraat 27)

Shopping

Chocolate Line

FOOD

23 🔒 Map p52, B2

Bruges has 50 chocolate shops, but just five where chocolates are handmade on the premises. Of those,

---

Understand
Belgian Brews

Belgian Beer is much more than a recipe for a good night out. Beer is to Belgium what wine is to neighbouring France – something to be savoured slowly, appreciating each brew's individual characteristics and flavours. Appreciating them all could take a while: it's estimated up to 1000 different beers are brewed nationwide. Each beer has its own unique glass embossed with the beer's logo (marking the level where the head starts) and is specially shaped to enhance the taste and aromas, meaning pouring techniques vary.

While monks in France are renowned for winemaking, in Belgium they're devoted to beer. Smooth gold- and dark-coloured Trappist beers – packing 6% to 12% alcohol content – have been made for centuries by Trappist (Cistercian) monks. These days, the monks' average age is 70, and there are few new recruits, prompting fears for the beers' future. For now, three abbeys still brew in Flanders.

And, in the same way that France has champagne, Belgium has its traditional vintage, the lambic (*lambiek* in Dutch). Like champagne, these sparkling beers take up to three years to make. The secret is wild micro-organisms that inhabit the cold air around the beer, causing spontaneous fermentation. The most popular lambic is the cider-style *gueuze* (pronounced 'gerze'). They're an acquired taste, but beginners can try fruit lambics that are sweetened with more palatable cherry or raspberry.

Easier to wash down are pale, cloudy white beers (*witbier* in Dutch, *bière blanche* in French), such as Bruges' Brugs Tarwebier. These are great iced with lemon in warm weather, unlike many of the country's beers, which are actually best drunk at room temperature.

Belgium also boasts golden ales; abbey beers (strong, full-flavoured ales, such as Leffe, using original abbey recipes); Vlaams Rood ('Flemish Red' beers, aged in wooden barrels); and sour-tasting Oud Bruin ('Old Brown' beers that blend young and old brews, with a secondary fermentation in the bottle).

the Chocolate Line, is the brightest and best. Wildly experimental flavours by 'shock-o-latier' Dominique Persoone include bitter Coca-Cola, Cuban cigar, wasabi and black olive, tomato and basil; it also sells pots of chocolate body paint (complete with a brush). (www.thechocolateline.be; Simon Stevinplein 19; per kg €50; ⊘10am-6pm)

Zucchero   FOOD

24 🔒 Map p52, C2

A fabulous new sweet shop with eye-popping fuchsia decor. It sells umpteen varieties of fudge and candies, plus ice cream to go. Check out the candy sticks being hand-chopped by the young owners. (☏050 33 39 62; www.confiserie-zucchero.be; Mariastraat 18; ⊘10am-6pm Tue-Sat, 11am-6pm Sun)

De Striep   COMICS

25 🔒 Map p52, C3

Look for Thibaut Vandorselaer's wonderful illustrated guides at this colourful comic shop. There's also a comprehensive collection in Dutch, French and English. You'll find Bruges-set comics by the counter. (☏050 33 71 12; www.striepclub.be; Katelijnestraat 42; ⊘10am-12.30pm & 1.30-7pm Tue-Sat, 2-6pm Sun)

Mille-Fleurs   HOMEWARES

26 🔒 Map p52, D1

A cornucopia of Flemish tapestries machine-made near Wetteren. Worth a browse if you want to take a piece of Belgium home with you. It also sells throws, tapestry cushions, runners and doilies, and bags and purses. (☏050 34 54 54; www.millefleurstapestries.com; Wollestraat 33)

Zilverpand   SHOPPING CENTRE

27 🔒 Map p52, B1

Covered shopping area between Steenstraat and Noordzandstraat. (btwn Steenstraat & Noordzandstraat)

Top Sights
Belgian Coast

Getting There

🚆 A rapid train trip (or 50-minute bike ride) brings you to the 66km of coastline

🚋 Coastal trams stop at 70 seaside towns and villages.

Virtually all of Belgium's 66km coastline is fronted with a superbly wide, hard-sand beach. However, while some remnant sand dunes survive, the coast is predominantly backed by resorts, with belle époque De Haan being a highpoint. Out of season many towns feel deserted, but with its regular events and conventions, hub-town Ostend manages to keep a lively vibe year-round. The Paul Delvaux Museum is a homage to the surrealist artist, while the wackily named Plopsaland appeals to kids.

Beach-goers on the coast, Ostend

Don't Miss

Ostend

Bustling Ostend is primarily a domestic seaside resort. Along its remarkably wide sandy beach is a spacious promenade surveyed by shoulder-to-shoulder tea rooms. But it's also rich in history. As a fortified port it was ravaged by a four-year siege (1600–1604) as the last 'Belgian' city to refuse Spanish reconquest. Later it bloomed as one of Europe's most stylish seaside resorts. Most of that style disappeared during WWII when German occupying forces (re)built the remarkable Atlantikwall sea defences.

Belle Époque De Haan

Prim and proper De Haan (Le Coq) is Belgium's most compact and engaging beach resort. Fanciful half-timbered hotels and tasteful eateries and shops form an appealing knot around a cottage-style former tram station, which houses the tourist office. East of the La Pontinière park, Normandiëlaan leads west to an area of whitewashed and thatched mansions in lanes that undulate gently through dunes.

Paul Delvaux Museum

The Delvaux Museum occupies a pretty whitewashed cottage that was home and studio to Paul Delvaux (1897–1994), one of Belgium's most famous surrealist artists; explore his warped take on perspective and dreamy evocations of the 'poetic subconscious'. From the Koksijde/St-Idesbald tram stop walk west along the main road towards De Panne, then follow signs inland and left, around 1km total. The museum has a delightful garden cafe.

Plopsaland

A Kusttram stop between Adinkerke and central De Panne serves Plopsaland, a major kids' theme park based around wonderfully named Belgian TV characters Wizzy, Woppy and Plop the gnome.

www.delvauxmuseum.com

www.plopsa.be/plopsaland-de-panne/en

☑ Top Tips

▶ Every settlement offers a wide selection of accommodation, but heavy bookings mean finding a room can still be hard in summer.

▶ Head just inland to Veurne to see a classic medieval Belgian square.

▶ Make a musical odyssey in Ostend, where Marvin Gaye wrote 'Sexual Healing'.

✕ Take a Break

Tearoom restaurants covering a wide range of styles and prices stand side-by-side along the promenade west of Ostend's Kursaal. There are plenty more seafood restaurants along Visserkaai. Market day is Thursday.

Explore

Grand Place & Ilôt Sacré

Brussels' heart beats in the Grand Place, ringed by gold-trimmed, gabled houses built by merchant guilds, and flanked by the 15th-century Gothic town hall. In the 12th century this was used as a marketplace; the names of the surrounding lanes still evoke herbs, cheese and poultry. Nearby are glass-covered shopping arcades and Brussels icon the Manneken Pis.

The Sights in a Day

☼ Where else to start your day but the **Grand Place** (p66), identifying the splendid guild houses and visiting the **Brussels City Museum** (p74). Next, head to the **Musée du Costume et de la Dentelle** (p72) to see handmade Brussels lace bedecking lovely historic gowns and shawls. If you're feeling flush, break for lunch at **La Maison du Cygne** (p78).

☼ Take a turn around the glorious **Galeries St-Hubert** (p75) in the footsteps of Victor Hugo. Cartoon fans will love the **Centre Belge de la Bande Dessinée** (p68), while architecture buffs can marvel at the Horta-designed department store it is housed in. Have a predinner beer at the irresistible **Théâtre Royal de Toone** (p83).

☾ Enjoy a leisurely supper and listen to some live piano at **Le Cercle des Voyageurs** (p76) – while you're here, take a short detour to see the small but unmistakable **Manneken Pis** (p72). Head to the **Music Village** (p82) for more live jazz, or order a half-and-half at **Le Cirio** (p78). Return to the Grand Place at night, to see it in floodlit glory.

◉ Top Sights

Grand Place (p66)

Centre Belge de la Bande Dessinée (p68)

♥ Best of Brussels

Best for Haute Cuisine
L'Ogenblik (p76)

La Maison du Cygne (p78)

Sea Grill (p77)

Best Live Music Bars
Le Cercle des Voyageurs (p76)

Music Village (p82)

Art Base (p84)

Best Cinemas
Actor's Studio (p84)

Cinéma Galeries (p83)

Getting There

Ⓜ **Metro** This central area is easily accessed via metro stations De Brouckère, Gare Centrale and Rogier.

🚋 **Premetro** The premetro station Bourse is a couple of blocks northwest of the Grand Place.

Top Sights
Grand Place

The magnificent Grand Place is one of the world's most unforgettable urban ensembles. Oddly hidden, the enclosed cobblestone square is only revealed as you enter on foot from one of six narrow side alleys: Rue des Harengs is the best first approach. The focal point is the magnificently spired 15th-century city hall, but each of the fabulous antique guildhalls (mostly 1697–1705) has a charm of its own. Most are unashamed exhibitionists adorned with fine baroque gables, gilded statues and elaborate guild symbols.

⊙ Map p70, C6

Ⓜ Gare Centrale

Grand Place

Don't Miss

Hôtel de Ville

Built between 1444 and 1480, the splendid Hôtel de Ville was almost the only building on the Grand Place to escape bombardment by the French in 1695. The creamy stone facade is covered with Gothic gargoyles and reliefs of nobility. The intricate tower soars 96m, topped by a gilded statue of St Michel, Brussels' patron saint.

Maison du Roi

This fanciful feast of neogothic arches, verdigris statues and minispires is bigger, darker and nearly 200 years younger than the surrounding guildhalls. Once a medieval bread market, the current master-piece dates from 1873 and nowadays houses the Brussels City Museum (p74), featuring old maps, architectural relics and paintings. Don't miss Pieter Brueghel the Elder's 1567 *Cortège de Noces* (Wedding Procession), and the 760-odd costumes – including an Elvis suit – belonging to Manneken Pis (p72).

Houses & Guildhalls

Among the Grand Place's gorgeous buildings and guildhalls are the following, listed by street number and guild: (5; Archers) **La Louve** – the golden phoenix rising from the ashes signifies the rebirth of the Grand Place after the bombardment; (6; Boatmen) **Le Cornet** has a stern-shaped gable; (9; Butchers) **Le Cygne** hosted Karl Marx in 1847; (10; Brewers) **L'Arbre d'Or** features hop plants climbing the columns – two basement rooms house a small Brewery Museum.

Dukes of Brabant Mansion

The mansion consists of six 1698 houses behind a single palatial facade reworked in 1882. Had the imperial governor had his way after 1695, the whole square would have looked like this.

☑ Top Tips

▶ Tours depart from the tourist office daily: 10am for a bike tour (p157) or 3pm for a city walking tour with the same company.

▶ There are guided tours of the Hôtel de Ville in English.

▶ Alive with classic *cafés* (pubs), the square takes on different auras at different times. Try to visit more than once, and don't miss a look at night when the scene is magically (and tastefully) illuminated.

▶ There's a flower market on Monday, Wednesday and Friday mornings.

▶ The Grand Place also hosts everything from Christmas fairs to rock concerts, to the extraordinary biennial 'flower carpet' (August).

✕ Take a Break

Take time out for biscuits, tea and ice cream at historic Dandoy (p76), just off the Grand Place.

Top Sights
Centre Belge de la Bande Dessinée

Belgium's national Comic Strip Centre is a studious look at the evolution of comics: how they're made, seminal artists and their creations, and contemporary comic-strip artists. Even if you're not excited by the 'ninth art', do peep inside Victor Horta's 1906 light-filled glass-and-steel textile warehouse in which the museum is housed.

👁 Map p70, E3

Belgian Comic Strip Centre

www.comicscenter.net

Rue des Sables 20

adult/concession €10/6.50

Centre Belge de la Bande Dessinée

Don't Miss

The Invention of the Comic Strip
This exploration of the history of the ninth art goes right back to mosaics, and makes a compelling case that the manuscripts of medieval monks – with their divided story strips and speech bubbles – were the first cartoons. The evolution continues through to the picture stories of 19th-century New York newspapers.

The Museum of the Imagination
This gallery focuses on Belgium's favourite cartoon character: Tintin, created by the great Hergé. It posits Tintin as a visually blank 'everyman' who can transform himself into a granny, a turbaned Indian or a white-bearded sage. Volatile Captain Haddock is by contrast a volcano of uncontrolled emotion, while the narrative is often sparked by the misunderstandings and bizarre actions of Professor Calculus. Among other Belgian artists explored in less depth, you may want to pause over the little blue creatures created by Peyo: the Smurfs.

Horta's building
Designed as a department store in 1906, the lovely building features a swirling tiled floor, slim metal pillars, girders and grills and light filtered through a glass ceiling. As you enter, a model of Tintin's red rocket gleams against the pale stone; to the right is a small exhibition about the construction, decline and restoration of the building.

☑ Top Tips

▶ You don't have to pay an entrance fee to enjoy the central hallway or to drink a coffee (€2.20) at the attached cafe.

▶ Temporary exhibitions on the top floor show international comic-strip art.

▶ Don't miss the shop, which steers clear of merchandise and focuses on books, including *Sarkozik* – a satire on the ex-French president, plus the Smurfs and Tintin.

▶ Should you want more reading matter – albeit in French – there's a comic-book library next door.

✕ Take a Break

The adjoining cafe, **Brasserie Horta** (www.brasseriehorta.be; Rue des Sables 20; mains €14-18; ⊙noon-3pm Tue-Sun; Ⓜ Rogier), is an attractive place serving Belgian standards.

Rogier Ⓜ Ⓗ

200 m
0.1 miles

Ⓔ   Ⓓ Ⓝ

R de Malines

R des Cendres

R de la Blanchisserie

R du Damier

Ⓗ 58

Blvd Adolphe Max

R St Pierre

R Neuve

R aux Choux

Pl des
Martyrs

R St-Michel

R d' Argent

R des Boiteux

Centre Belge
de la Bande
Dessinée Ⓞ

R des Sables

R du Marais

R du Meiboom

d de Berlaimont

45 Ⓗ

Montagne aux
erbes Potagères

22 Ⓧ

Blvd Emile Jacqmain

R de l'Épargne

R du Pélican

R aux Fleurs

Pont-Neuf

R de la Fiancée

R du Finistère

Ⓟ

50 Ⓞ

R du Cirque

R Van der Elst

R des Hirondelles

Pl de
Brouckère

Ⓒ

60 Ⓗ

Ⓗ 38

Pl de
Brouckère

Ⓜ
De Brouckère

R du Fossé aux Loups

54 Ⓗ

R des
Princes

Pl de la
Monnaie

R de la Reine

R Léopold

R de l'Éc

R de l'Évêque

des

Ⓑ

51 Ⓞ

Q aux Pierres de Tailles

R du Canal

R de Laeken

R des Augustins

Blvd Anspach

R des Halles

R de l'Évêque

Ⓖ

R Grétr

For reviews see

Ⓞ Top Sights	p66
Ⓞ Sights	p72
Ⓧ Eating	p75
Ⓓ Drinking	p78
Ⓔ Entertainment	p82
Ⓖ Shopping	p86

Pl du
Béguinage

R du Grand-Hospice

R du Rouleau

Ste-Catherine

Pl du
Samedi

STE-CATHERINE

Ⓐ

59 Ⓗ

Q au Bois à Brûler

Q aux Briques

Marché aux
Poissons

Ⓧ16
Ⓗ34

R du Peuplier

R du Bois à Brûler

36 Ⓗ

Pl Ste-
Catherine

R J Plateau

R du Marché
aux Poule

R de la Vierge Noire

37 Ⓗ

R Melsens

Pl Ste-
Catherine

R Ste-Catherine

Ⓧ15

31 Ⓥ

Sights

Musée du Costume et de la Dentelle
MUSEUM

1 Map p70, C6

Lace-making has been one of Flanders' finest crafts since the 16th century. While *kloskant* (bobbin lace) originated in Bruges, *naaldkant* (needlepoint lace) was developed in Italy but was predominantly made in Brussels. This excellent museum reveals lace's applications for under- and outerwear over the centuries, as well as displaying other luxury textiles in beautifully presented changing exhibitions. Ask for an English-language booklet. (Costume & Lace Museum; 02-213 44 50; www.museeducostumeetdeladentelle. be; Rue de la Violette 12; admission €4, with Brussels Card free; ⊙10am-5pm Thu-Tue; MGare Centrale)

Manneken Pis
MONUMENT

2 Map p70, B7

Rue Charles Buls – Brussels' most unashamedly touristy shopping street, lined with chocolate and trinket shops – leads the hordes three blocks from the Grand Place to the Manneken Pis. This fountain-statue of a little boy taking a leak is comically tiny and a perversely perfect national symbol for surreal Belgium. Most of the time the statue's nakedness is hidden beneath a costume relevant to an anniversary, national day or local event: his ever-growing wardrobe is partly displayed at the **Maison**

du Roi (Musée de la Ville de Bruxelles; Grand Place; MGare Centrale). (cnr Rue de l'Étuve & Rue du Chêne; MGare Centrale)

Jeanneke Pis
MONUMENT

3 Map p70, C5

Squatting just off Rue des Bouchers, this pigtailed female counterpart of the Manneken Pis is the work of sculptor Denis Adrien Debouvrie, who installed her here in 1985. She's usually partly obscured by locked iron gates. (www.jeannekepisofficial.be; Impasse de la Fidélité; MGare Centrale)

Musée du Cacao et du Chocolat
MUSEUM

4 Map p70, B6

Exhibits at Brussels' museum of cocoa and chocolate give you a quick rundown of chocolate's history in Europe, along with chocolate's anti-ageing and antidepressant properties. A couple of small treats along the way include a tasting at the praline-making demonstration. Better yet are the museum's occasional one-hour praline-making courses – call for details. (02-514 20 48; www.choco-story-brussels.be; Rue de la Tête d'Or 9; adult/under 12yr/concession €6/3.40/5; ⊙10am-4.30pm Tue-Sun; MGare Centrale or Bourse)

Underpant Museum
GALLERY

5 Map p70, C7

One of the city's weirder offerings, located upstairs from the Dolle Mol *café*. Not a museum in any real

Understand

Mural-Spotting

Over 40 comic-strip murals currently enliven alleys and thoroughfares throughout the old city centre, with more added year after year. Moseying past a few of these bright murals makes a great excuse to explore less-visited neighbourhoods. Some favourites:

Tibet & Duchateau (Rue du Bon Secours 9; Ⓜ Bourse) Very effectively sees a life-sized figure teetering towards a trompe l'œil window.

Josephine Baker (Rue des Capucins 9; Ⓜ Porte de Hal) One of the most distinctive Marolles murals – slinky chanteuse Josephine, with a leopard on a lead, shakes hands with a rotund monk. Behind, both in the mural and in real life, is the looming dome of the Palais de Justice. Baker performed in Brussels in the 1920s and '30s, and famously kept a leopard as a pet.

Tintin (Rue de l'Étuve; Ⓜ Bourse) The most famous of Belgium's characters.

Broussaille (Rue du Marché au Charbon; Ⓜ Bourse) Depicts a young couple arm-in-arm. The original 1991 version showed a couple of very ambiguous sex that the neighbouring gay establishments used to promote the quarter. However, a 1999 repaint seemed to give the black-haired figure a more feminine hairstyle, earrings and (slightly) bigger breasts. Creeping homophobia or honest mistake? Nobody knows.

Peeping Policeman (Rue Haute; Ⓜ Louise) Hergé character uses the terrace end brilliantly for a little spying.

Manneken Pis Displaced (Rue de Flandre; Ⓜ Ste-Catherine) A tetchy-looking Manneken Pis gazes up at his pediment, from which he has been displaced by a grinning, peeing bear.

FC de Kampioenen (Rue du Canal; Ⓜ Ste-Catherine) This bright and dynamic mural features not a football club, but a parade of characters based on a TV series that ran from 1990 to 2011. The show was turned into a comic strip by Hec Leemans in 1997.

sense, it displays collages created by filmmaker and artist Jan Bucquoy, incorporating the underpants of Belgian celebs. The entrance fee gets you a postcard featuring your pant artwork of choice. (Musée du Slip; www.janbucquoy.be/janbucquoy/Musee_du_slip.html; Dolle Mol, Rue des Éperonniers 52; admission €1; ◔2-6pm Sun; Ⓜ Gare Centrale)

Fondation Jacques Brel

MUSEUM

6 ◉ Map p70, C7

Chansonnier Jacques Brel (1929–78) made his debut in 1952 at a cabaret in his native Belgium and shot to fame in Paris, where he was a contemporary of Édith Piaf and co, though his songs continued to hark back to the bleak 'flat land' of his native country. This dedicated archive centre and museum, set up by his daughter, contains more than 100 hours of footage and another 100 of audio recordings, plus thousands of photographs and articles.

Dedicated fans can also take the audio walking tour. (☏02-511 10 20; www.jacquesbrel.be; Place de la Vieille Halle aux Blés 11; adult/student €5/3.50, walk with audioguide €8, walk & museum €10; ◔noon-6pm Tue-Sat, plus Mon Aug; Ⓜ Gare Centrale)

Musée de la Brasserie

MUSEUM

7 ◉ Map p70, C6

Brussels' brewery museum is authentic in the sense that it occupies the basement of the brewers' guildhall and has some 18th-century brewing equipment. But visitors are often disappointed at its small size and the lack of any actual brewing taking place (though you do get a beer at the end). To see a real brewery in action, head to the Cantillon Brewery's Musée Bruxellois de la Gueuze (p123). (☏02-511 49 87; www.beerparadise.be; Grand Place 10; admission €5; ◔10am-5pm daily Apr-Nov, noon-5pm Sat & Sun Dec-Mar; Ⓜ Gare Centrale or 🚌Bourse)

Brussels City Museum

MUSEUM

8 ◉ Map p70, C6

Old maps, architectural relics and paintings give a historical overview of the city. Don't miss Pieter Brueghel the Elder's 1567 *Cortège de Noces* (Wedding Procession). (Musée de la Ville de Bruxelles; ☏02-279 43 50; www.museedelavilledebruxelles.be; adult/concession/Brussels Card €4/3/free; ◔10am-5pm Tue-Sun, to 8pm Thu; Ⓜ Gare Centrale, 🚌Bourse)

Q Local Life

Where to Eat Waffles

Locals get 'real' waffles at **Mokafé** (☏02-511 78 70; Galerie du Roi; waffles from €3; ◔7.30am-11.30pm; Ⓜ De Brouckère), an old-fashioned cafe under the glass arch of the Galeries St-Hubert. It's a little timeworn inside, but wicker chairs in the beautiful arcade provide you with a good view of passing shoppers. Note that traditional waffles have 20 squares, and are dusted with icing sugar rather than loaded with cream.

Galeries St-Hubert

ARCHITECTURE

9 ⊙ Map p70, D5

When opened in 1847 by King Léopold I, the glorious Galeries St-Hubert formed Europe's very first shopping arcade. Many enticing shops lie behind its neoclassical glassed-in arches flanked by marble pilasters. Several eclectic *cafés* spill tables onto the gallery terrace, safe from rain beneath the glass roof. The arcade is off Rue du Marché aux Herbes. (www.galeries-saint-hubert.com; Ⓜ Gare Centrale)

Rue des Bouchers

STREET

10 ⊙ Map p70, C5

Uniquely colourful Rue and Petite Rue des Bouchers are a pair of narrow alleys jam-packed with pavement tables, pyramids of lemons and iced displays of fish and crustaceans. It's all gloriously photogenic, but think twice before eating here, as the food standards are generally poor (an exception is the classic Aux Armes de Bruxelles, (p78).

Bourse

BUILDING

11 ⊙ Map p70, B5

The Bourse is Belgium's 1873 stock-exchange building. It's closed to visitors, but you can enjoy its grandiose neoclassical facade, brilliantly festooned with friezes and sculptures, reclining nudes, lunging horses and a multitude of allegorical figures. Some of the work is by Rodin, then a young

apprentice sculptor. (Place de la Bourse; 🚊 Bourse)

Bruxella1238

ARCHAEOLOGICAL SITE

12 ⊙ Map p70, B5

Bruxella1238 is the scanty remains of a Franciscan convent that was bombarded into ruins in 1695. Most of the site is visible by peeping through the glass windows set into the pavement roughly outside Le Cirio *café* (p78). (admission €4; ⊙ tours in English 10.15am 1st Wed of month)

Église St-Nicolas

CHURCH

13 ⊙ Map p70, B5

Near the Bourse, this pint-sized church is as old as Brussels itself. What really makes it notable is its virtual invisibility – the exterior is almost totally encrusted with shops. Appropriately enough, it's dedicated to the patron saint of merchants. (Church of St-Nicolas; Rue au Beurre 1; ⊙ 8am-6.30pm Mon-Fri, 9am-6pm Sat, 9am-7.30pm Sun; 🚊 Bourse)

Eating

Arcadi

BRASSERIE €

14 ✖ Map p70, D5

The jars of preserves, beautiful cakes and fruit tarts of this classic and charming bistro entice plenty of Brussels residents, as do well-priced meals such as lasagne and steak, all served nonstop by courteous staff. With a nice location on the edge of the Galeries

St-Hubert, this is a great spot for an indulgent, creamy hot chocolate. (☎02-511 33 43; Rue d'Arenberg 1b; snacks from €5; ⏱7am-11pm; Ⓜ Gare Centrale)

Cremerie de Linkebeek   DELI €

15   Map p70, A4

Brussels' best *fromagerie* (cheese shop) was established in 1902 and retains its original glazed tiles. It still stocks a beguiling array of cheeses, which you can also try on crunchy baguettes with fresh salad, wrapped in blue-and-white-striped paper ready to take to a nearby bench. (☎02-512 35 10; Rue du Vieux Marché aux Grains 4; ⏱9am-3pm Mon, to 6pm Tue-Sat; Ⓜ Ste-Catherine)

Henri   FUSION €€

16   Map p70, A3

In an airy white space on this street to watch, Henri concocts tangy fusion dishes such as tuna with ginger, soy and lime, artichokes with scampi, lime and olive tapenade, or Argentine fillet steak in parsley. There's an astute wine list, and staff who know their stuff. (☎02-218 00 08; www.restohenri.be; Rue de Flandre 113; mains €16-20; ⏱noon-2pm Tue-Fri & 6-10pm Tue-Sat; Ⓜ Ste-Catherine)

L'Ogenblik   FRENCH €€€

17   Map p70, C5

It may be only a stone's throw from Rue des Bouchers, but this timeless bistro with its lace curtains, resident cat, marble-topped tables and magnificent wrought-iron lamp feels a world away. They've been producing French classics here for more than 30 years, and the expertise shows. Worth the price for a special meal in the heart of town. (☎02-511 61 51; www.ogenblik.be; Galerie des Princes 1; mains €23-29; ⏱noon-2.30pm & 7pm-midnight; ⓐ Bourse)

Le Cercle des Voyageurs   BRASSERIE €€

18   Map p70, B7

Delightful bistro featuring globes, an antique-map ceiling and a travel library. If your date's late, flick through an old *National Geographic* in your colonial leather chair. The global brasserie food is pretty good, and there are documentary screenings and free live music: piano jazz on Tuesday and experimental on Thursday. Other gigs in the cave have a small entrance fee. (☎02-514 39 49; www.lecercledesvoyageurs.com; Rue des Grands Carmes 18; mains €15-21; ⏱11am-midnight; 📶; ⓐ Bourse, Anneessens)

Dandoy   BISCUITS €

19   Map p70, B5

Established in 1829, Brussels' best-known *biscuiterie* (biscuit shop) has five local branches, this one with an attached tearoom. The chocolate for Dandoy's choc-dipped biscuits is handmade by Laurent Gerbaud. (☎02-511 03 26; www.maisondandoy.com; Rue au Beurre 31; ⏱9.30am-7pm Mon-Sat, 10.30am-7pm Sun; Ⓜ Bourse)

Musée du Costume et de la Dentelle (p72)

Brasserie de la Roue d'Or

BELGIAN €€

20 Map p70, C6

Cosy in a cramped Parisian-bistro sort of way, this place serves excellent if somewhat pricey Belgian food. Wall murals and ceiling clouds pay homage to the city's surrealist artists. (02-514 25 54; Rue des Chapeliers 26; mains €15-28; noon-12.30am, closed Jul; M Gare Centrale)

Kokob

ETHIOPIAN €€

21 Map p70, A7

A warmly lit Ethiopian bar/restaurant/ cultural centre at the bottom of Rue des Grands Carmes, where well-explained dishes are best shared, eaten from and with pancake-like *injera* – it's a place to visit in a group rather than on your own. Traditional coffee ceremonies are held on Wednesday evening and noon to 3pm Sunday. (02-511 19 50; www.kokob.be; Rue des Grands Carmes 10; menus per person from €20; 6-11pm Mon-Thu, noon-3pm & 6-11pm Fri-Sun; Annessens, Bourse)

Sea Grill

SEAFOOD €€€

22 Map p70, D4

You'd be hard pressed to find a more unlikely setting for Brussels' finest seafood than this '80s-styled place. But at the Michelin-starred Sea Grill, Yves Mattagne and his team create just that in the open kitchen. Try the

Low-hanging awnings strung with fairy lights, oyster stands on the cobblestones and aproned waiters hustling for business cram narrow Rue des Bouchers, which intersects Galeries St-Hubert. Yes, this is tourist central, and due to the generally poor food standards, locals steer clear. An exception is the classic, expensive **Aux Armes de Bruxelles** (☎02-511 55 98; www.auxarmesde-bruxelles.com; Rue des Bouchers 13; mains €19-57; ☺noon-11.15pm Tue-Sun; 🚊Bourse).

Brittany lobster, crushed and extracted in an antique solid-silver lobster press (one of only four in the world) and prepared at your table. (☎02-212 08 00; www.seagrill.be; Radisson SAS Royal Hotel Brussels, Rue du Fossé aux Loups 47; ☺noon-2pm & 7-10pm, closed mid-Jul–mid-Aug; Ⓜ De Brouckère)

La Maison du Cygne   BELGIAN €€€

23 🍴 Map p70, C6

Gastronomic Belgo-French seasonal cuisine is served in this sophisticated restaurant on the 2nd floor of a classic 17th-century guildhall. Book way ahead to score one of the few tables with a Grand Place view. For something slightly less formal, try its 1st-floor **Ommegang Brasserie** (mains €16-27; ☺noon-2.30pm & 6.30-10.30pm Mon-Sat). (☎02-511 82 44; www.greatmomentsin-brussels.be; Rue Charles Buls 2; mains €38-65, menus from €65; ☺noon-2pm & 7-10pm Mon-Fri, 7-10pm Sat; Ⓜ Gare Centrale)

Osteria a l'Ombra   ITALIAN €€

24 🍴 Map p70, C6

Take a tiny, tiled-walled 1920s shop-house. Keep the classic decor, wooden shelf-holders and cashier booth. Insert stools and a narrow communal table. Serve great fresh pasta and see if the customers finally communicate. Perhaps...at least with the farewell grappa. (Rue des Harengs 2; pastas €9-13, mains €11-16; ☺noon-2.30pm & 6.30-11.30pm Mon-Sat; Ⓜ Gare Centrale)

Drinking

Goupil le Fol   BAR

25 🍷 Map p70, C7

Overwhelming weirdness hits you as you acid-trip your way through this sensory overload of rambling passageways, ragged old sofas and inexplicable beverages mostly based on madly fruit-flavoured wines (no beer is available). Unmissable. (☎02-511 13 96; Rue de la Violette 22; ☺9pm-5am; Ⓜ Gare Centrale)

Le Cirio   PUB

26 🍷 Map p70, B5

This sumptuous 1886 *grand café* (large, elegant pub) dazzles with polished brasswork and aproned waiters, yet prices aren't exorbitant and coiffured *mesdames* with small dogs still dilute the gaggles of tourists. The house speciality is a half-and-half mix of still and sparkling wines (€3.20). (Rue de la Bourse 18; ⏱10am-midnight; 🚊Bourse)

Falstaff PUB

27 🚇 Map p70, B5

The interior of this *grand café* is an astonishing festival of century-old, art nouveau stained glass and fluidity designed by Horta disciple Houbion. A wide range of meals is available. (www. lefalstaff.be; Rue Henri Maus 17; ⏱10am-1am; 🚊Bourse)

À la Mort Subite PUB

28 🚇 Map p70, D5

An absolute classic unchanged since 1928, with lined-up wooden tables, arched mirror panels and entertainingly brusque service. (📞02-513 13 18; www.alamortsubite.com; Rue Montagne aux Herbes Potagères 7; ⏱11am-1am Mon-Sat, noon-midnight Sun; Ⓜ Gare Centrale)

À la Bécasse PUB

29 🚇 Map p70, B5

Hidden almost invisibly down a body-wide alley-tunnel, the Bécasse has long rows of tables that give it a certain Brueghelesque quality, even though it's 'only' been operating since 1877. The unusual speciality is *panaché*, a jug of Timmermans lambic mixed with fruit beer or faro to make it more palatable. It's not to everyone's taste. (www.alabecasse.com; Rue de Tabora 11; ⏱11am-midnight, to 1am Fri & Sat; Ⓜ Gare Centrale)

Au Soleil BAR

30 🚇 Map p70, A7

This old clothes shop has been converted into a shabby-chic bar with good beats and surprisingly inexpensive drinks given its status as a favourite for posers in shades. (📞02-513 34 30; Rue du Marché au Charbon 86; ⏱10.30am-late; 🚊Bourse)

BarBeton BAR

31 🚇 Map p70, A4

Typical of the new array of hip but relaxed Brussels bars, with a tiled floor and unpolished wood furnishings. It's good for an early breakfast, and there's a lavish €15 brunch on Sunday. Cocktail happy hour is 7pm to 8pm Thursday, there's an *aperitivo* (pre-dinner drinks) buffet from 6pm to 8pm Friday and there are DJs from 10pm till late on Saturday. (www.barbeton.be; Rue Antoine Dansaert 114; ⏱8am-late; 📶; Ⓜ Ste-Catherine)

La Fleur en Papier Doré PUB

32 🚇 Map p70, B8

The nicotine-stained walls of this tiny *café*, adored by artists and locals, are covered with writings, art and scribbles by Magritte and his surrealist pals, some of which were reputedly traded for free drinks. *'Ceci n'est pas un musée'*, quips a sign on the door reminding visitors to buy a drink and not just look around. (www.goudblommekeinpapier.be; Rue des Alexiens 53; ⏱11am-midnight Tue-Sat, to 7pm Sun; 🚊Bruxelles Central)

Understand
Being Belgian

'Nothing works here, and still it works. That's Belgium.' Statements by locals such as these sum up Belgians' acceptance of – even pride about – their country's seeming absurdity at times (the fact that it ticked along quite nicely without a federal government for months for example). Belgians are, on the whole, an innovative, optimistic bunch with an easy-going outlook.

Citizens often identify themselves as Flemish (Dutch-speaking) or Walloon (French-speaking) first, and Belgian second. Moreover, Brussels is a vibrant hub of multiculturalism, whose population includes many other European nationalities as well as Moroccans, Turks and Africans (especially from the former Belgian Congo).

Religion also plays a part in identity and day-to-day life, including politics and education. Roughly 75% of Belgium's population is Roman Catholic, and despite church attendance plummeting, traditions endure. Protestant communities also maintain a strong presence, and the capital has a significant Muslim population.

When it comes to moral freedom, Belgium is a world leader. Same-sex couples have been able to wed legally in Brussels since 2003, and have the same rights as heterosexual couples, including inheritance and adoption. Euthanasia was legalised in 2002.

For all its quirks and contrasts, Belgium is refreshingly uncomplicated in terms of social interaction, with few pitfalls for visitors. The main issue to watch for outside of Brussels is language – the capital itself is officially bilingual, but despite being geographically in Flanders, it's predominantly French-speaking. In Bruges, if you don't attempt Dutch you should speak English and not French.

As far as customs go, men and women, and women and women, greet each other with three kisses on the cheek (starting on the left) when meeting for the first time: after that it's usually just one kiss (again on the left). Men shake hands with men. And, unlike in neighbouring France and the Netherlands, shopkeepers won't generally greet you when you enter their premises. This isn't unfriendliness, but rather to avoid being seen as giving the hard sell – something that's shunned by Belgians, who are unassuming by nature. But contrasts are ever-present: one of the national symbols is the Manneken Pis (p72), unabashedly baring himself to the world.

Bourse (p75)

Fontainas Bar
BAR

33 Map p70, A7

The ripped black-vinyl seats, '60s tables and light fittings, and cracked tiles of this loud and ultratrendy bar provide the backdrop for locals reading newspapers by day, until the party cranks up again come nightfall. (📞02-503 31 12; Rue du Marché au Charbon 91; 🕙10am-late Mon-Fri, 11am-late Sat & Sun; 🚋Bourse)

Walvis
BAR

34 Map p70, A3

Sounds from soul to punk to progressive rock (live, DJs or just through the speakers) play at this ubercool bar, where entry's free, the atmosphere buzzes and the staff is great. (📞02-219 95 32; www.cafewalvis.be; Rue Antoine Dansaert; 🕙11am-2am Mon-Thu & Sun, to 4am Fri & Sat; ⓂSte-Catherine)

Le Cercueil
BAR

35 Map p70, C6

Grungy, all-black madness with coffins for tables and lit mainly by UV. (The Coffin; Rue des Harengs 10-12; beer from €2.80; 🕙4pm-late Mon-Tue, 1pm-late Fri-Sun; 🚋Bourse)

Madame Moustache
CLUB

36 Map p70, A3

Cute Ste-Catherine club with a retro, burlesque feel. It hosts funk all-nighters and swing nights, plus garage

and DJ sets. (www.madamemoustache.
be; Quai au Bois à Brûler 5-7; ⏱9pm-4am
Tue-Sun; Ⓜ Ste-Catherine)

La Vilaine
CLUB

37 🚊 Map p70, B4

Brand-new club in an art deco building with a louche speakeasy vibe and
leather armchairs. They play electroni-
ca and hip hop to a young, fun crowd.
(www.clublavilaine.be; Rue de la Vierge Noire
10; cover €8-12; ⏱10pm-4am Wed-Sat; Ⓜ De
Brouckère)

Local Life
Beer Witness

Sample the local brews at **Moeder
Lambic Fontainas** (www.moederlam-
bic.com; Place Fontainas 8; ⏱11am-1am
Sun-Thu, to 2am Fri & Sat; 🚊 Anneessens, Bourse), which, at the last
count, served 46 artisanal beers,
in a contemporary rather than old-
world setting: walls are bare brick
and hung with photos, and booths
are backed with concrete.

If you prefer to span the globe
when drinking, visit **Délirium Café**
(www.deliriumcafe.be; Impasse de la
Fidélité 4a; ⏱10am-4am Mon-Sat, to
2am Sun; Ⓜ Gare Centrale), with its
barrel tables, beer-tray ceilings
and over 2000 world beers – to
which they've recently added a
rum garden, a taphouse and the
Floris Bar (from 8pm), serving
hundreds of jenevers (Dutch gins),
vodkas and absinthes. No wonder
it's lively.

Métropole Café
BAR

38 🚊 Map p70, C3

The magnificently ornate belle-
époque interior easily justifies the
hefty drink prices, though, curiously,
a large number of punters still decide
to sit on its comparatively unappeal-
ing street terrace. (Hotel Métropole; www.
metropolehotel.com; Place de Brouckère
31; beer/coffee/waffles from €3.80/3.80/7;
Ⓜ De Brouckère)

A l'Image de
Nostre-Dame
PUB

39 🚊 Map p70, C5

Down a tiny hidden alley from Rue du
Marché aux Herbes 5, Nostre-Dame
has an almost medieval feel but retains
a genuine local vibe. Magical...except
for the toilets. (⏱noon-midnight Mon-Fri,
3pm-1am Sat, 4-10.30pm Sun; 🚊 Bourse)

Celtica
BAR

40 🚊 Map p70, B5

Lewd, loud, central and – most impor-
tantly – cheap: just €1 for a beer. (www.
celticpubs.com/celtica; Rue de Marché aux
Poulets 55; 🚊 Bourse)

Entertainment

Music Village
JAZZ

41 ⭐ Map p70, B6

Polished 100-seat jazz venue housed
in two 17th-century buildings with
dinner (not compulsory) available

À la Mort Subite (p79)

from 7pm and concerts starting at 8.30pm, 9pm at weekends. The performers squeeze onto a small podium that's visible from any seat. Bookings advised. (📞02-513 13 45; www.themusic-village.com; Rue des Pierres 50; cover €7.50-20; ⏰from 7pm Wed-Sat; 🚇Bourse)

Théâtre Royal de Toone   THEATRE

42 ⭐ Map p70, C5

Eight generations of the Toone family have staged classic puppet productions in the Bruxellois dialect at this endearing marionette theatre, a highlight of any visit to Brussels. Shows are aimed at adults, but kids love them too. (📞02-511 7137; www.toone.be; Petite Rue des Bouchers 21; adult/child €10/7; ⏰variable, typically 8.30pm Thu & 4pm Sat; 🚇Gare Centrale)

Cinéma Galeries   CINEMA

43 ⭐ Map p70, C5

Inside the graceful glassed-over Galeries St-Hubert, this art deco beauty concentrates on foreign and art-house films. An authentic Brussels movie experience. (📞02-514 74 98; www.arenberg.be; Galerie de la Reine 26; 🚇Bourse)

L'Archiduc   JAZZ

44 ⭐ Map p70, A4

This intimate, split-level art deco bar has been playing jazz since 1937. It's an unusual two-tiered circular space

ALAN COPSON/GETTY IMAGES ©

Rue des Bouchers (p75)

that can get incredibly packed but remains convivial. You might need to ring the doorbell. Saturday concerts (5pm) are free; Sunday brings in international talent and admission charges vary. (📞02-512 06 52; www.archiduc.net; Rue Antoine Dansaert 6; beer/wine/cocktails €2.50/3.60/8.50; ⏱4pm-5am; 🚇Bourse)

Art Base   LIVE MUSIC

45 ⭐ Map p70, E3

One of the best little venues in town for music fans with eclectic tastes. It resembles someone's living room, but the programming is first rate, and it's worth taking a punt on Greek *rebetiko*, Indian classical music,

chamber concerts, Argentine guitar or whatever else is playing. (📞02-217 29 20; www.art-base.be; Rue des Sables 29; ⏱Fri & Sat; 🚇Rogier)

Actor's Studio   CINEMA

46 ⭐ Map p70, C5

This intimate and tucked away three-screen cinema, a little hard to locate just off touristy Petite Rue des Bouchers, shows art-house flicks as well as some mainstream reruns, and has a tiny bar. Try to catch a movie here – it's one of the city's indie treasures and the tickets are cheaper than in the big movie houses. (📞02-512 16 96;

www.actorsstudio.cinenews.be; Petite Rue des Bouchers 16; ⛄Bourse)

AB
LIVE MUSIC

47 ⭐ Map p70, A6

The AB's two auditoriums are favourite venues for midlevel international rock bands and acts such as Jools Holland and Madeleine Peyroux, plus plenty of home-grown talent. The ticket office is located on Rue des Pierres. There's a good on-site bar-restaurant that opens at 6pm (bookings essential). (Ancienne Belgique; ✆02-548 24 00; www.abconcerts.be; Blvd Anspach 110; ⛄Bourse)

Théâtre du Vaudeville
THEATRE

48 ⭐ Map p70, C6

Cabarets, concerts and various theatre productions take place at this old theatre within the Galeries St-Hubert. Program leaflets are available in the foyer inside the arcade. (✆02-512 57 45; Galeries St-Hubert, Galerie de la Reine 13-15; Ⓜ Gare Centrale)

Théâtre Royal de la Monnaie/Koninklijke Muntschouwburg
OPERA, DANCE

49 ⭐ Map p70, C4

Belgium was born when an opera at this grand venue inspired the 1830 revolution. Nowadays it primarily mounts contemporary dance, and classic and new operas. (✆02-229 13 72; www.lamonnaie.be; Place de la Monnaie; Ⓜ De Brouckère)

Théâtre National
THEATRE

50 ⭐ Map p70, D1

The francophone community's rectilinear glass theatre. (✆02-203 41 55; www.theatrenational.be; Blvd Émile Jacqmain 111-115; Ⓜ Rigier)

Q Local Life

Jazz in Brussels

Jazz has a special place in Belgium, the home of Adolphe Sax (inventor of the saxophone), Romany guitar king Django Reinhardt and octogenarian harmonica whiz Toots Thielemans, who is still going strong as a performer. Along with Music Village (p82), other long established and much-loved venues include the **Jazz Station** (✆ 02-733 13 78; jazzstation.be; Chaussée de Louvain 193a; ⊙exhibitions 11am-7pm Wed-Sat, concerts 6pm Sat & 8.30pm some weeknights; Ⓜ Madou); on rue Antoine Dansaert, **L'Archiduc** (p83) and **Sounds** (✆02-512 92 50; www.soundsjazzclub. be; Rue de la Tulipe 28; ⊙8pm-4am Mon-Sat; Ⓜ Porte de Namur) in Ixelles. The **Brussels Jazz Marathon** (www.brusselsjazzmarathon.be) is held in venues across the city in May, while the **Skoda Jazz Festival** (www.skodajazz.be) goes countrywide in October and November.

Koninklijke Vlaamse Schouwburg
THEATRE

51 ⭐　Map p70, B1

Behind a restored Renaissance facade, the state-of-the-art Royal Flemish Theatre mounts edgy dance and theatre productions, occasionally in English. (☎02-210 11 12; www.kvs.be; Rue de Laeken 146; Ⓜ Yser)

Shopping

Boutique Tintin
BOOKS

52 🔒　Map p70, C6

No prizes for guessing the star of this comic shop, which stocks albums galore and cute merchandise. (☎02-514 51 52; en.tintin.com; Rue de la Colline 13; ⏰10am-6pm Mon-Sat, 11am-5pm Sun; 🚇; Ⓜ Gare Centrale)

Catherine
FOOD

53 🔒　Map p70, B6

A traditional and welcoming grocery in the heart of town, specialising in artisanal cheeses, several of them organic. You'll also find cured meats and condiments – all the perfect basis of a simple supper if you're self-catering. (☎02-512 75 64; Rue du Midi 23; ⏰9am-6pm Mon-Sat; 🚊 Bourse)

Sterling Books
BOOKS

54 🔒　Map p70, D4

English-language bookshop with comfy sofas and a kids' play area.

(☎02-223 62 23; www.sterlingbooks.be; Rue du Fossé aux Loups 38; ⏰10am-7pm Mon-Sat, noon-6.30pm Sun; Ⓜ De Brouckère)

De Biertempel
DRINK

55 🔒　Map p70, C5

As its name states, this shop is a temple to beer, stocking upwards of 700 brews along with matching glasses and other booze-related merchandise. For more ordinary beers and for bulk purchases, make like the locals and go to the supermarket. (☎02-502 19 06; Rue du Marché aux Herbes 56b; ⏰9.30am-7pm; 🚊 Bourse)

Neuhaus
FOOD

56 🔒　Map p70, D5

Belgium's original – established in 1857. This stunning flagship store has stained-glass windows and sumptuous displays. (☎02-512 63 59; www.neuhaus. be; Galerie de la Reine 25; chocolate per kilogram €52; ⏰10am-8pm Mon-Sat, to 7pm Sun; Ⓜ Gare Centrale)

Planète Chocolat
FOOD

57 🔒　Map p70, B6

Both moulds and chocolates are made on site. At 4pm Saturday and Sunday there are praline-making demonstrations explaining chocolate's development, culminating in a chance for visitors to create their own chocolates. (☎02-511 07 55; www. planetechocolat.be; Rue du Lombard 24; chocolate per kilogram €50; ⏰11am-6pm Mon & Sun, 10.30am-6.30pm Tue-Sat; 🚊 Bourse)

Belgian waffle

City 2
SHOPPING CENTRE

58 🔒 Map p70, E1

This modern shopping mall has all the usual chain-store suspects, but it's a good bet for electronic gear from FNAC, which also sells events tickets. In the mall's basement you'll find a post office, and a better-than-average food court – try Ganesh for fantastic Indian samosas, curries and naan breads. (Rue Neuve 123; Ⓜ Rogier)

Micro Marché
HANDICRAFTS

59 🔒 Map p70, A1

You'll find alternative and affordable handmade crafts at boho Micro Marché, which adjoins the convivial Traveller's Café. (www.micromarche.com; Quai à la Houille 9; ⏰4-9pm Fri, 11am-7pm Sat & Sun; Ⓜ Ste-Catherine)

Passage du Nord
SHOPPING ARCADE

60 🔒 Map p70, C3

Passage du Nord's array of quality boutiques makes this vaulted glass arcade a good spot to escape the rain. (off Rue Neuve; Ⓜ De Brouckère)

Explore

Royal Quarter Museums

The majestic Royal Quarter takes in the Palais Royal, the grandiose Palais de Justice (pictured), and the Mont des Arts, where Brussels' premier museums are housed in some of the city's most magnificent buildings, all a few steps from each other. Antique shops, tearooms and chocolate boutiques cluster around the Place du Grand Sablon, while graceful churches and the elegant Parc de Bruxelles add to the area's rarefied air.

The Sights in a Day

☀ Start your day at the **Musées Royaux des Beaux-Arts** (p90), seeing the work of the Flemish Primitives, Brueghel's *Fall of Icarus* and the adjoining **Musée Magritte** (p91). Head to one of the cafés on the Place du Grand Sablon for lunch, or pick up a picnic at **Claire Fontaine** (p100) and enjoy it in the Place du Petit Sablon.

☀ Be sure to peek into the **Église Notre-Dame du Sablon** (p96) while you're here. Then make a beeline for the **Musée des Instruments de Musique** (p924), housed in the art nouveau Old England Building. Take a tea break in the rooftop *café* (pub), or head downhill for the famous chocolates and a cuppa at **Laurent Gerbaud** (p100). To find out more about Belgium's history, check out the **Musée BELvue** (p98), located in an elegant former palace.

☾ For dinner, enjoy brasserie food at the charming **Le Perroquet** (p101), or for something more up-market, be sure to book ahead for **Les Brigittines** (p99). Later, take in a high-brow concert at **BOZAR** (p103), or enjoy the live piano accompaniment of a silent classic at the **Cinematek** (p103).

👁 Top Sights

Musées Royaux des Beaux-Arts (p90)

Musée des Instruments de Musique (p92)

💙 Best of Brussels

Best Shops for Chocolate
Mary (p104)

Pierre Marcolini (p103)

Laurent Gerbaud (p100)

Best Speciality Museums
Musée des Instruments de Musique (p92)

Magritte Museum (p91)

Musée BELvue (p98)

Best Churches
Église Notre-Dame du Sablon (p96)

Cathédrale des Sts-Michel & Gudule (p96)

Getting There

Ⓜ Metro Stops Louise and Porte de Namur on lines 2 and 6 are best for the Place du Sablon, while Gare Central, on lines 1 and 5, is best for the Mont des Arts.

🚋 Tram 92, 93 and 94 pass through the district.

Top Sights
Musées Royaux des Beaux-Arts

The prestigious Royal Museums of Fine Arts incorporate both the Musée d'Art Ancien (ancient art) and the Musée d'Art Moderne (modern art). Among the many highlights are collections of the Flemish Primitives, the Brueghels (especially Pieter the Elder) and Rubens in the Musée d'Art Ancien; and works by surrealist Paul Delvaux and fauvist Rik Wouters in the subterranean Musée d'Art Moderne. The complex also celebrates the country's favourite surrealist son in the purpose-built Musée René Magritte.

◉ Map p94, C5

Royal Museums of Fine Arts

www.fine-arts-museum.be

Rue de la Régence 3

adult/6-25yr/Brussels Card €8/2/free, with Magritte Museum €13

Main hall, Musées Royaux des Beaux-Arts

Don't Miss

The Flemish Primitives

The work of these 15th-century masters is wonderfully represented in the gallery: look out for Roger Van der Weyden's *Pietà* with its hallucinatory dawn sky; Dieric Bouts' dramatic tableau depicting the torments of an unjustly accused husband and his faithful wife, *Justice of the Emperor Otto* and the richly textured *Madonna with Saints* by the anonymous Master of the Legend of St Lucy.

The Brueghels

While Pieter the Elder was the greatest of this family of artists, his sons' work echoed his humorous and tender scenes, where the central narrative of the painting often has to be sought out among a wealth of lively rustic detail. The most famous example is the *Fall of Icarus*, where the hero's legs disappearing into the waves are overshadowed by the figure of an unconcerned ploughman and a jaunty ship.

Rubens & His Followers

Antwerp painter Pieter Paul Rubens specialised in fleshy religious works, of which there are several colossal examples here. But his lesser-known works, such as his *Studies of a Negro's Head* show he was also a master of psychological portraiture. In this section, look out too for Anthony Van Dyck's contemplative human studies, Cornelius De Vos' charming family portrait, and works by Rembrandt and Frans Hals.

Musée Magritte

This adjoining **museum** (www.musee-magritte-museum.be) offers a chronological exploration of the artist's work, including surreal and playful photos and films. In his famous canvases, motifs of spheres, pipes and birds appear repeatedly, as does the image of his wife Georgette.

☑ **Top Tips**

▶ On the first Wednesday of the month, this and many other Brussels museums are free from 1pm. Don't plan to see any Brussels museum on a Monday – it'll be firmly closed.

▶ Consider visiting the Musée Magritte separately, as it merits at least two hours – you can buy a joint ticket and return another day.

▶ The museum also hosts acclaimed temporary exhibitions, for which there's an extra charge.

▶ Check out the small sculpture garden, to the left as you face the building.

✕ **Take a Break**

The **museum cafe** (🕙10am-5pm Tues-Fri, 11am-6pm Sat & Sun) is a pricey but pleasant spot serving sandwiches, salads and cakes, with a terrace punctuated with statues overlooking the rooftops.

Top Sights
Musée des Instruments de Musique

This ground-breaking museum is a celebration of music in all its forms and a repository for more than 2000 historic instruments. The emphasis is on listening, with auditory experiences around every corner, from arcane shepherds' bagpipes to Chinese carillons to harpsichords. The cumulative effect is very moving, mapping human experience through the infinite variety of our music. The ornate, elongated art nouveau Old England building is a superb setting.

👁 Map p94, C4

Rue Montagne de la Cour 2

adult/concession €8/6

🕓9.30am-5pm Tue-Fri, 10am-5pm Sat & Sun

Ⓜ Gare Centrale, Parc

Musée des Instruments de Musique

Don't Miss

Sound Lab
The exhibits in this dimly lit gallery are numbered, with each number corresponding to a point on the soundtrack you hear via headphones. Sounds range from a 16th-century church bell chiming midnight to a 19th-century bird organ and 20th-century Hammond organ blues. Among the artefacts is a barrel organ with wooden figures that, when animated, enact various grisly teeth-pulling operations.

Traditional Instruments
This gallery contains every instrument you've ever heard of, and then some. You can appreciate the aesthetic qualities of actual instruments from around the world as well as – via the headphones – musical mastery, from the intricacies of the Indian sitar to the otherworldly wail of Tibetan horns to Congolese drums and harps. One of the weirdest sights and sounds is the Mardi Gras bear mask from Limbourg in Belgium, sitting alongside rough-hewn instruments and with accompanying primitive chants.

Western Art Music
A precious collection of Western wind, string and keyboard instruments. The early variations on pianos, painted with delicate flowers and pastoral scenes, are among the most attractive items on display; look out too for the huge serpent-headed bassoons. As with the other galleries, plug in your headphones to listen as well as look.

The Old England Building
The art nouveau Old England building is much of a highlight as the museum itself. This former department store was built in 1899 by Paul Saintenoy and has a panoramic rooftop cafe and terrace.

☑ Top Tips

▶ Headphones are essential for a visit, but don't worry if you don't speak French or Flemish – all you'll hear is music.

▶ There is no labelling in English, so collect a handout at the entrance to each gallery.

▶ The museum shop has a great collection of CDs: it closes for an hour from 12.30pm.

▶ To see the building but not the museum, take the lift to the top floor and make your way back down via the stairs.

▶ There are regular concerts in the museum's recital hall: check the What's On section of the website.

✕ Take a Break

Head to the top floor for spectacular views framed by wrought-iron curlicues at **Cafetéria du Mim** (☏02-502 95 08; www.restomim. com; Rue Montagne de la Cour 2; meals €12-16; ☺10am-4.30pm, closed Mon).

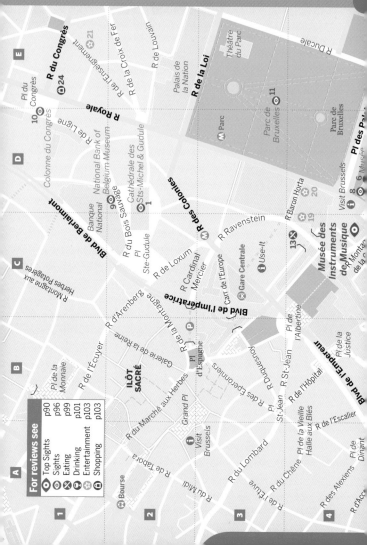

For reviews see
- ● Top Sights   p90
- ◉ Sights   p96
- ✖ Eating   p99
- ㊟ Drinking   p101
- ✪ Entertainment   p103
- ⊞ Shopping   p103

MATONGÉ

Chaussée de Wavre

Chaussée d'Ixelles

R Longue Vie
R de la Paix
R Solvay

Trône Ⓜ

Pl du Trône

R du Champ de Mars

R Bréderode

R de Edimbourg

Square du Bastion

Porte de Namur Ⓜ

R de Namur

R de Stassart

R du Béger

Ave de la Toison d'Or

R des Chevaliers

R des Drapiers

R Cap Crespel

Royaux des Ⓞ Beaux-Arts

Royale

Palais Royal Ⓞ 7

Pl du Grand Sablon 15 ✗

Église Notre-Dame du Sablon 2 Ⓞ

Ⓞ 25 16 ✗

Place du Petit Sablon 3 Ⓞ

Ⓞ 23

R Leb

R des U

R de Rollebeek

Église Notre-Dame de la Chapelle Ⓞ 4

Pl de la Chapelle

R de la Régence

R Van Moer

R Watteeu

R C

R Ernest Allard

R des Minimes

R du Temple Hanssens ✗ 17

Pl Poelaert

R Notre Seigneur

R Haute

R des U

12 ✗

R Blaes

Ⓞ 18

Pl Breugel

✗ 22

Jardin d'Egmont

R aux Laines

R du Grand-Cerf

Bld de Waterloo

Palais de Justice 5 Ⓞ

Ave Louise

Pl Louise

Louise Ⓜ

Ave de la Toison d'Or

Pl J Jacobs

R aux Laines

R de la Prévoyance

✗ 14

Ⓝ

0.2 miles
400 m

Sights

Cathédrale des Sts-Michel & Gudule
CHURCH

1 ◎ Map p94, D2

Host to coronations and royal weddings, Brussels' grand, twin-towered cathedral bears at least some resemblance to Paris' Notre Dame. Begun in 1226, construction took 300 years. Stained-glass windows flood the soaring nave with light, while column-saints brandish gilded tools. An enormous wooden pulpit by Antwerp artist Hendrik Verbruggen sees Adam and Eve driven out of Eden by skeletons. To climb the cathedral towers (€5, 10am on the second Saturday of each month), sign up a day or two ahead. (www.cathedralisbruxellensis.be; Place Sainte-Gudule; admission free, treasury €1, crypt

€3; ⏱7am-6pm Mon-Fri, 8.30am-6pm Sat, 2pm-6pm Sun; Ⓜ Gare Centrale)

Église Notre-Dame du Sablon
CHURCH

2 ◎ Map p94, C5

The Sablon's large, flamboyantly Gothic church started life as the 1304 archers' guild chapel. A century later it had to be massively enlarged to cope with droves of pilgrims attracted by the supposed healing powers of its Madonna statue. The statue was procured in 1348 by means of an audacious theft from an Antwerp church – apparently by a vision-motivated husband-and-wife team in a rowing boat. It has long since gone, but a boat behind the pulpit commemorates the curious affair. (Rue de la Régence; ⏱9am-6pm Mon-Fri, 10am-6pm Sat & Sun; Ⓜ Porte de Namur)

Place du Petit Sablon
PARK

3 ◎ Map p94, C6

About 200m uphill from Place du Grand Sablon, this charming little garden is ringed by 48 bronze statu-ettes representing the medieval guilds. Standing huddled on a fountain plinth like two actors from a Shakespear-ean drama are Counts Egmont and Hoorn, popular city leaders who were beheaded in the Grand Place in 1568 for defying Spanish rule. The site of Egmont's grand former residence lies behind. (Ⓜ Porte de Namur)

Cathédrale des Sts-Michel & Gudule organ

Église Notre-Dame de la Chapelle

CHURCH

4 ⊙ Map p94, A5

Brussels' oldest surviving church now curiously incorporates the decapitated tower of the 1134 original as the central section of a bigger Gothic edifice. Behind the palm-tree pulpit, look on the wall above a carved confessional to find a small memorial to 'Petro Brevgello', ie artist Pieter Brueghel the Elder, who once lived in the nearby Marolles. (Place de la Chapelle; admission free, pamphlet €3; ⊙9am-7pm Jun-Sep, to 6pm Oct-May; 🚊Anneessens)

Palais de Justice

HISTORIC BUILDING

5 ⊙ Map p94, A7

Larger than St Peter's in Rome, this 2.6-hectare complex of law courts was the world's biggest building when it was constructed (1866–83). While the labyrinthine complex is undoubtedly forbidding, it is not easy to secure. Indeed, in several high-profile cases criminals have absconded from its precincts. Behind the building a terrace offers wide panoramas over the Brussels rooftops, with the Atomium and Koekelberg Basilica the stars of the skyline show. A glass **elevator** (Place Brueghel, Rue de l'Epée; admission free; ⊙7.30am-11.45pm) leads down to

Statue in Parc de Bruxelles

the earthy Marolles district. (Place Poelaert; **M**Louise, 🚌92, 94)

Musée BELvue
MUSEUM

6 ⊙ Map p94, D4

Take a chronological audio tour through the airy stuccoed interior of this former royal residence to explore Belgium's history from independence to today, brought to life by exhibits and film footage. Among the artefacts is the jacket worn by Albert I when he died in a climbing accident in 1934. In summer, the restaurant has tables in the pretty garden. (📞07-022 04 92; www.belvue.be; Place des Palais 7; adult/concession €6/5; ⊙9.30am-5pm Tue-Fri, 10am-6pm Sat & Sun; **M**Parc)

Palais Royal
PALACE

7 ⊙ Map p94, D5

These days Belgium's royal family lives at **Laeken** (Royal Estate; 🚌53 from **M** Bockstael), but this sturdy 19th-century palace remains its 'official' residence. One unique room has had its ceiling iridescently clad with the wing cases of 1.4 million Thai jewel beetles by conceptual artist Jan Fabre. You'll also see contemporary royal portraits. It's only open to visitors in summer. (📞02-551 20 20; www.monarchy.be; Place des Palais; admission free; ⊙10.30am-4.30pm Tue-Sun late Jul-early Sep; **M**Parc)

Coudenberg
ARCHAEOLOGICAL SITE

8 ⊙ Map p94, D4

Coudenberg Hill (now Place Royale) was the site of Brussels' original 12th-century castle. Over several centuries this was transformed into one of Europe's most elegant and powerful palaces, most notably as the 16th-century residence of Holy Roman Emperor Charles V. Around the palace, courtiers and nobles in turn built fine mansions. The vast complex was destroyed in a catastrophic 1731 fire, but beneath street level the basic structure of the palace's long-hidden lower storeys remains.

Whole stretches of the medieval street layout are now discernible, though little atmosphere remains. The subterranean site is entered from Musée BELvue and you emerge near the Old England Building. (www.couden-berg.com; adult/under 26yr/Brussels Card €6/5/free; ⊙9.30am-5pm Tue-Fri, 10am-6pm Sat & Sun; MParc)

National Bank of Belgium Museum
MUSEUM

9 ◉ Map p94, D2

Unexpectedly absorbing, the National Bank Museum is far more than just a coin collection. Well-presented exhibits trace the very concept of money all the way from cowrie shells to credit cards. (☎02-221 22 06; www.nbbmuseum.be; Blvd de Berlaimont 3; admission free; ⊙10am-5pm Mon-Fri; MGare Centrale)

Colonne du Congrès
MONUMENT

10 ◉ Map p94, D1

Brussels' 25m-tall version of Nelson's Column is an 1850s monolith topped by a gilded statue of King Léopold I. It commemorates the Belgian constitution of 1831. The four female figures around its base represent the four constitutionally upheld freedoms of religion, association, education and the press. The last of these encouraged Victor Hugo, Karl Marx and others to visit Belgium back when such freedoms were much more restricted in other parts of Europe.

Between two bronze lions, an eternal flame honours Belgian victims of the two world wars. (Place du Congrès; MMadou)

☑ Top Tip
Discount Tickets

If you're planning a night out, your first stop should be the tourist office on Rue Royale 2. Here a ticket desk (open 12.30pm to 5.30pm) sells heavily discounted tickets for concerts, theatre and cinema, from the grand BOZAR to tucked away art-house movie theatres.

Parc de Bruxelles
OUTDOORS

11 ◉ Map p94, E3

Brussels is well endowed with outlying forests and parklands, but in the inner city it's a different story. The largest central patch of greenery is the Parc de Bruxelles, an old, formal park flanked by the Palais Royal and the Palais de la Nation. Laid out under the auspices of the dukes of Brabant, it's dotted with classical statues and framed by trees with mercilessly trellised branches. Lunchtime office workers, joggers and families with kids love it in summer. (Pl des Palais; 🚌92, 93 or 94, 🚊Parc)

Eating

Les Brigittines
FRENCH, BELGIAN €€

12 🍽 Map p94, A5

Offering grown-up eating in a muted belle époque dining room, Les Brigittines dishes up traditional French and Belgian food. Its classic (and very meaty) dishes include veal cheek, pigs' trotters and steak tartare. Staff are knowledgeable about local beer and artisanal wines, and can advise on pairing these with your food. (☏02-512 68 91; www.lesbrigittines.com; Place de la Chapelle 5; mains €16-24; ⏱noon-2.30pm & 7-10.30pm Mon-Fri, noon-2.30pm & 7-11pm Sat; Ⓜ Louise)

Laurent Gerbaud
CAFE €

14 🍴 Map p94, C4

A bright and welcoming cafe with big picture windows that's perfect for lunch or a coffee if you're between museums. Don't leave without trying the wonderful chocolates, which count as healthy eating in the world of Belgian chocs – they have no alcohol, ad-

---

☑ Top Tip

Mussels in Brussels

Steaming cast-iron pots of mussels (*mosselen* in Dutch, *moules* in French) appear on restaurant tables everywhere. They're traditionally cooked in white wine, with variations such as *à la Provençal* (with tomato) and *à la bière* (in beer and cream), and are accompanied by fries. Mussels were previously only eaten during months with an 'r' in their name, to be assured of their freshness, but modern cultivation techniques now mean mussels in July onwards are considered OK. Never eat any that haven't opened properly once they've been cooked.

---

ditives or added sugar. Friendly owner Laurent also runs chocolate-tasting and -making sessions. (☏02-511 16 02; www.chocolatsgerbaud.be; Rue Ravenstein 2; snacks from €5; ⏱7.30am-7.30pm; Ⓜ Parc)

Restobières
BELGIAN €€

14 🍴 Map p94, A7

Beer-based twists on typical Belgian meals served in a delightful if slightly cramped restaurant. The walls are plastered with bottles, grinders and countless antique souvenir biscuit tins featuring Belgian royalty. Try the *carbonade* (beer-based hot pot) or *lapin aux pruneaux* (rabbit with prunes). (☏02-502 72 51; www.restobieres.eu; Rue des Renards 9; mains €12-22, menus €18-38; ⏱noon-3pm & 7-11pm Tue-Sun; Ⓜ Louise)

Le Village de la Bande Dessinée
BRASSERIE €

15 🍴 Map p94, B5

Cartoon-themed burgers, Belgian specialities, bagels, salads and milkshakes all designed to appeal to kids. Red-and-white gingham tablecloths add to the jolly vibe, but there's also a serious collection of cartoons and memorabilia in the bookshop, and a gallery hung with original Hergé drawings. (☏02-523 13 23; comicscafe.be; Place du Grand Sablon 8; snacks from €6; ⏱11am-11pm Tue-Sun; 🚋 Louise)

Claire Fontaine
DELI €

16 🍴 Map p94, B5

Just off Place du Grand Sablon, this is a tiny but atmospheric tile-floored

Église Notre-Dame du Sablon (p96)

épicerie (grocery), fragrant with spices and home-cooked dishes – there's a small kitchen at the back. It's perfect for a nutritious and filling takeaway sandwich or quiche, or you can stock up on oils, wine and boxes of *pain d'épices* (spiced biscuits). (☎ 02-512 24 10; Rue Ernest Allard 3; Ⓜ Porte de Namur)

Le Perroquet   CAFE €

17 🍴 Map p94, B6

Perfect for a drink, but also good for a simple bite (salads and variations on croques-monsieurs), this art nouveau cafe with its stained glass, marble tables and timber panelling is an atmospheric, inexpensive stop in an area that's light on such places. Popular with expats. (Rue Watteeu 31; light meals €8-14; ⊙ noon-1am; Ⓜ Porte de Namur)

Drinking

Brasserie Ploegmans   PUB

18 🍺 Map p94, A6

This classic local hostelry with old-fashioned mirror-panelled seats and 1927 chequerboard flooring is well regarded for its typical Bruxellois meals. (www.ploegmans.be; Rue Haute 148; mains €13.50-18.50; ⊙ noon-2.30pm Tue-Fri & 6-10pm Tue-Sat, closed Aug; Ⓜ Louise)

Understand
Belgian Independence & the Congo

Belgium has a long history of colonisation, beginning in the mid-16th century when Brussels was proclaimed capital of the Spanish Netherlands. French attempts to dominate Europe meant many wars were fought in this buffer land; fighting came to a head during the War of Spanish Succession (1701–13), which saw the Spanish Netherlands handed to the Austrians. The mighty Austrian Hapsburgs ruled for 81 years, until the French reclaimed the region in 1794. When, in 1815, Napoleon Bonaparte was defeated at the Battle of Waterloo near Brussels, the United Kingdom of the Netherlands, incorporating the Netherlands, Belgium and Luxembourg, was created.

Belgium finally achieved independence via an unlikely revolution of opera-goers. The opera – staged in Brussels in August 1830 and concerning Naples' uprising against the Spanish – inspired the bourgeois audience to join the workers who were demonstrating outside against the Dutch rulers. Together, opera-goers and workers stormed the town hall, and a new nation was created.

At the Conference of London in January 1831, Belgium was officially declared a neutral state and Léopold of Saxe-Coburg Gotha became King Léopold I of Belgium; the country now celebrates his coronation on 21 July as its National Day holiday. The ensuing years saw the beginnings of Flemish nationalism, with growing tension between Dutch and French speakers eventually leading to the language partition in 1898.

Léopold II came to the throne on his father's death in 1865. He was committed to transforming the tiny country into a strong nation and, in 1885, personally acquired a huge slice of central Africa – an area 70 times larger than Belgium. Over the following 25 years, five to eight million Congolese died due to legally permitted atrocities committed in the rubber plantations. In 1908, in the face of mounting international pressure, the king was compelled to cede possession of the Congo to the Belgian state, which continued to hold the territory until 1960. For more on the Belgian Congo, a good place to start is *King Leopold's Ghost* by Adam Hochschild.

Entertainment

BOZAR

LIVE MUSIC

19 ⭐ Map p94, C4

This celebrated classical-music space is home to the National Orchestra and Philharmonic Society. From the outside, the Horta-designed 1928 art deco building is bold rather than enticing, but Henri Le Bœuf Hall is considered to be one of the five best venues in the world for acoustic quality. BOZAR also hosts major art and science exhibitions. (www.bozar.be; Palais des Beaux-Arts, Rue Ravenstein 23; Ⓜ Gare Centrale)

Cinematek

CINEMA

20 ⭐ Map p94, D4

In a wing of the BOZAR cultural centre, the modern and stylish Cinematek includes a little museum where you can browse archives and memorabilia. The real highlight, though, is the program of silent films screened nearly every day at the cinema, with live piano accompaniment. There's also an impressive program of art-house movies. (🖉02-507 83 70; www.cinematheque.be; Rue Baron Horta 9; Ⓜ Gare Centrale)

Cirque Royal

THEATRE

21 ⭐ Map p94, E1

This converted indoor circus is now a venue for dance, operetta, classical and contemporary music. (🖉02-218 20 15; www.cirque-royal.org; Rue de l'Enseignement 81; Ⓜ Madou)

Théâtre Les Tanneurs

THEATRE

22 ⭐ Map p94, A6

Sitting on the edge of the Marolles, this theatre is known for dynamic drama and dance. (🖉02-512 17 84; www.lestanneurs.be; Rue des Tanneurs 75; Ⓜ Louise)

Shopping

Pierre Marcolini

FOOD

23 🔒 Map p94, B5

Rare chocolate beans, experimental flavours (eg tea) and designer black-box packaging make Marcolini's pralines Belgium's trendiest and most expensive. (🖉02-512 43 14; www.marcolini.be; Rue des Minimes 1; chocolate per kilogram €70; 🕙10am-7pm Sun-Thu, to 6pm Fri & Sat; Ⓜ Porte de Namur)

☑ Top Tip

Brussels Greeters

A great way of exploring a specific area or indulging in a passion for anything from *gueuze* (lambic) beers to Belgian politics, is to contact **Brussels Greeters** (www.brussels.greeters.be) two weeks before your trip. You fill in a simple online form and the coordinator sets you up with a local who will take you to relevant sights in the city, usually with stops for coffee and lunch along the way (trips take two to four hours). There is no charge for the service, and tips are not accepted.

The Brussels Capital Region comprises the only area in Belgium that's officially bilingual. Bilingualism means that communes, streets, train stations and so on frequently (but not always) have two names, such as the commune of Elsene (in Dutch), which is also known as Ixelles (in French). Street signs list the French, followed by the Dutch, such as 'Petite Rue de la Violette Korte Violetstraat' (Little Violet St). In French, *rue* (street) comes at the start, in Dutch *straat* is tacked on the end. Marolles signs contain three languages: French, Dutch and the Bruxellois dialect, resulting in mouthfuls such as Rue Haute Hoogstraat Op d'Huugstroet (High St). For simplicity, we've used the French names in this chapter.

Mary

FOOD

24 🔒 Map p94, E1

Supplies pralines to Belgium's royals plus the odd US president. (☎02-217 45 00; www.mary.be; Rue Royale 73; chocolate per kilogram €58; ☺10am-6pm Mon-Sat; Ⓜ Madou)

Sablon Antiques Market

MARKET

25 🔒 Map p94, B5

Over 100 vendors fill this stately square on weekends, selling crockery, crystal, jewellery, furniture, 18th-century Breton *faïence* (pottery) and other relics of bygone eras. Prices generally reflect the high quality of the goods for sale. (www.sablon-antiques-market.com; Place du Grand Sablon; ☺9am-6pm Sat, to 2pm Sun; Ⓜ Porte de Namur)

Statue and church on Place Royal (p98)

Explore

Parc du Cinquantenaire & EU Quarter

The EU Quarter doesn't have the best reputation, with its bland office blocks and thundering traffic. But there are plenty of sights to entice visitors, notably the museums grouped around leafy Parc Cinquantenaire. Some fine early-20th-century houses fringe Sq Marie-Louise and – of course – this is the heart of European politics, whether you see that as an enticement or a deterrent.

The Sights in a Day

Have a stroll round Parc Léopold, and if you're interested in EU politics, drop in to **EU Parliament** (p113) for the 10am tour. Otherwise, walk with the dinosaurs at the spectacular **Musée des Sciences Naturelles** (p113). Head to the Parc du Cinquantenaire, and take in a lofty view of the district from the arcade accessed via the military museum. Detour out of the park to see the glinting facade of the art nouveau **Maison Cauchie** (p109; pictured, left).

Break for lunch at the restaurant of the **Musée du Cinquantenaire** (p110). Give yourself lots of time to explore the richness of the museum, where you can explore several epochs in world art and artefacts. Either laze away some time in the park, or detour, via the star-shaped **Berlaymont Building** (p115), to **Square Marie-Louise** (p115), surrounded by tall and gracious apartment blocks, some from the art nouveau period.

This is not the greatest area for a night out, but **L'Atelier Europeén** (p116) is a swish dinner stop. Otherwise, lively Place Jourdan offers great restaurants, bars, pizzas and a classic *frites* (chips) stand.

Top Sights

Parc du Cinquantenaire (p108)

Musée du Cinquantenaire (p110)

Best of Brussels

Best for Haute Cuisine
Stirwen (p116)

L'Atelier Européen (p116)

Best Green Spaces
Parc du Cinquantenaire (p108)

Parc Léopold (p115)

Getting There

M Metro The best option to reach this area is the metro. The closest stop for the museums is Mérode, while to explore the EU sights head to Schuman. For Sq Marie-Louise get off at Maelbeek.

Top Sights
Parc du Cinquantenaire

For all the functionality of the EU district, the area retains graceful parks and squares, most notably the Parc du Cinquantenaire, flanking which are some standout museums showcasing everything from sarcophagi to Harley Davidsons. The Cinquantenaire itself is a triumphal arch reminiscent of Paris' Arc de Triomphe. It was designed to celebrate Belgium's 50th anniversary (*cinquantenaire* in French) in 1880, but it took so long to build that by that date only a temporary plaster version was standing. The full arch wasn't completed till 1905.

⊙ Map p112, E3

Rue de la Loi & Rue Belliard

Ⓜ Mérode

Cinquantenaire

Don't Miss

Maison Cauchie

The famous **Maison Cauchie** (☏02-733 86 84; www.cauchie.be; Rue des Francs 5; adult/child €5/free; ⏰10am-1pm & 2-5.30pm 1st Sat & Sun of each month, plus 6-8.30pm most evenings May-Aug) is an art nouveau treasure, whose stunning 1905 facade is lavishly adorned with stylised female figures, the rose motif picked up in a spherical window with a tiny balcony. Book ahead to see the fabulous sgraffito-adorned rooms upstairs.

Musée Royal de l'Armée et d'Histoire Militaire

One for military buffs, the **Musée Royal de l'Armée et d'Histoire Militaire** (Royal Museum of the Armed Forces and of Military History; ☏02-737 78 11; www.klm-mra.be; Parc du Cinquantenaire 3; admission free; ⏰10am-6pm Tue-Sun; Ⓜ Mérode) houses an extensive array of weaponry, uniforms, vehicles, warships, paintings and documentation dating from the Middle Ages through to Belgian independence and the mid-20th century.

Autoworld

Prior to WWII, Belgium had a thriving auto industry, and the coolest of car collections on display at **Autoworld** (www.autoworld.be; Parc du Cinquantenaire; adult/Brussels Card €9/free; ⏰10am-6pm Apr-Sep, to 5pm Oct-Mar; Ⓜ Mérode) is its legacy. Here you can see some 400 vehicles (Model T Fords, Citroen 2CVs and much more, through to the 1970s), housed in a stunning 1880 steel structure. Notice the Harley Davidson the present king gifted to Belgium's police force when he decided his biker days were over.

☑ Top Tips

▶ The top of the Cinquantenaire Arcade provides sweeping city views. You access it via the military museum either by steps or a lift.

▶ In summer, the arcade forms the curious backdrop to a drive-in cinema screen; check with the tourist board for program details.

▶ In the park itself, look out for the Pavillon Horta to the northwest. You won't find any of the architect's trademark motifs in this rather solid neoclassical structure, though: it was his first public commission.

✕ Take a Break

There's a great collection of cafes, restaurants and bars on Place Jourdan, including the city's most famous *frites* stand, Maison Antoine (p115).

Top Sights
Musée du Cinquantenaire

Few Belgians realise there's a treasure trove lurking within this cavernous antiquities museum. The astonishingly rich global collection ranges from Ancient Egyptian sarcophagi and Meso-American masks to Russian icons and wooden bicycles. Visually attractive spaces include the medieval stone carvings set around a neo-Gothic cloister and the soaring Corinthian columns (convincing fibreglass props) that surround a mosaic from Roman Syria.

⊙ Map p112, D3

www.kmkg-mrah.be

Parc du Cinquantenaire 10

adult/child/Brussels Card €5/€1.50/free

⊕9.30am-5pm Tue-Fri, from 10am Sat & Sun

Ⓜ Mérode

Exhibition room, Musée du Cinquantenaire

Don't Miss

Antiquity
The rich variety of antiquities ranges from ancient Egyptian treasures, including 10 mummies and sarcophagi, to a large collection of Belgian artefacts from the first human settlements in the region. The highlight, though, is the Roman Syrian gallery, where a large and vivid AD 415 mosaic depicts tigers being speared and lions being hunted down by dogs.

European Decorative Arts
Many people will make a beeline for the glorious art nouveau and art deco objects, whose display cases were designed by Victor Horta. There are also Romanesque, Renaissance and baroque galleries, and a changing collection of tapestries. A whole gallery is devoted to clocks and astronomical devices, and there's also a delightful assemblage of 35 painted sledges from the 1930s and '40s.

Non-European Civilisations
The scope of this section is impressive, taking in pre-Columbian art; Native American headdresses; Jainist, Hindu and Buddhist deities; Chinese ceramics; rare Islamic textiles; Byzantine art; and Coptic fabrics. Perhaps the most startling exhibit, though, is the woefully displaced Easter Island sculpture, a 6-tonne stone giant collected on a Franco-Belgian expedition in the 1930s.

Tintin Trail
The museum is a must for those on the Tintin trail: a goulish skeleton mummy inspired *The Seven Crystal Balls,* while the Arumba fetish in *The Broken Ear* was based on a wooden votive figure displayed in the galleries.

☑ Top Tips
▸ Labelling in Musée du Cinquantenaire is in French and Dutch, so the English-language audioguide (€3 extra) is worth considering.

▸ Have a clear idea of what you want to see, as the sheer scope can prove overwhelming. Individual highlights are flagged on the website in the 'masterpieces online' section.

▸ Admission is free on the first Wednesday of the month, after 1pm.

▸ On Sunday you can enjoy brunch at the museum restaurant before tackling the galleries.

▸ The museum shop sells scholarly guides to the gallery collections, as well as the usual memorabilia and gifts.

✕ Take a Break
The museum has an upmarket bistro, **Le Midi Cinquante** (☎02-735 87 54; mains €13-15; ⏰9.30am-4.30pm, closed Mon), whose terrace looks onto the park.

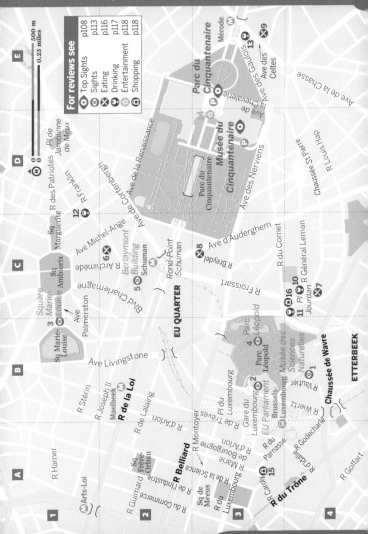

500 m
0.25 miles

Parc du Cinquantenaire

Musée du Cinquantenaire

Parc du Cinquantenaire

Merode Ⓜ

Ave des Gaulois

Ave des Celtes

Ave de la Chasse

Ave de Chevalerie

Ave des Nerviens

Chaussée St Pierre

R Louis Hap

Pl de Jambinne de Meux

R des Patriotes

R Franklin

Sq Marguerite

Ave de la Renaissance

Ave de Cortenbergh

Ave d'Auderghem

R du Cornet

R Général Leman

Sq Marie-Louise

Square Marie-Louise

Sq Ambiorix

Ave Palmerston

Blvd Charlemagne

Ave Michel-Ange

Berlaymont Building

R Archimède

Schuman Ⓜ

Rond-Point Schuman

R Breydel

R Froissart

R Jourdan

Pl Jourdan

EU QUARTER

Ave Livingstone

R Stévin

R Joseph II

Maelbeek Ⓜ

R de la Loi

R de Lalaing

R d'Arlon

Parc Léopold

Musée des Sciences Naturelles

ETTERBEEK

Chaussée de Wavre

R Hamer

Ⓜ Arts-Loi

R Guimard

Sq Frère-Orban

R de l'Industrie

R Belliard

R du Commerce

Sq de Meûs

R du Luxembourg

R de la Science

R Montoyer

Pl du Luxembourg

Gare du Luxembourg

Luxembourg Ⓜ

EU Parliament Brussels

Ave de Tervueren

Pl du Luxembourg

R de Trèves

R de Bourgogne

R d'Arlon

R Marie de Bourgogne

R Wiertz

R Vautier

R Parnasse

R Godecharle

R d'Italie

R du Trône

R Caroly

R Goffart

ETTERBEEK

1 2 3 4

A B C D E

Musée des Sciences Naturelles

Sights

Musée des
Sciences Naturelles   MUSEUM

1 ⊙ Map p112, B4

Thought-provoking and highly interactive, this museum has far more than the usual selection of stuffed animals. But the undoubted highlight is a unique 'family' of iguanodons – 10m-high dinosaurs found in a Hainaut coal mine in 1878. A computer simulation shows the mudslide that might have covered them, sand-boxes allow you to play dino hunter and multilingual videos give a wonderfully nuanced debate on recent palaeontology. (☏02-627

42 38; www.naturalsciences.be; Rue Vautier 29; adult/concession/child/Brussels Card €7/6/4.50/free; ⊙9.30am-5pm Tue-Fri, 10am-6pm Sat & Sun; ☒38 direction Homborch, departs from next to Gare Centrale, to De Meeus on Rue du Luxembourg)

EU Parliament   BUILDING

2 ⊙ Map p112, B3

Inside this decidedly dated blue-glass building (completed only just over a decade ago) political junkies can sit in on a parliamentary session in the huge debating chamber known as the hemicycle, or tour it when parliament's not sitting. Tours (using multilingual headphones) start at the visitor centre, attached

Understand

Belgian Break-Up

It's perhaps an irony that Belgium, with its central role in the – ideally – consensual politics of the European Commission and NATO, is linguistically and culturally at odds with itself. Nowhere is this split more evident than in bilingual Brussels, where there is real division between the numerically dominant French speakers and the proud Flemish residents.

In 2006, francophone public broadcaster RTBF interrupted programming with footage of a reporter outside the Royal Palace, claiming that Flanders had declared independence and King Albert had left the country. Only after half an hour did the program-makers admit the hoax, stating that they intended to demonstrate the importance of the ongoing political debate for the future of Belgium.

The question of whether Belgium will hold together or split apart is never far away. Brussels, with its geographical location in Flanders, its primary linguistic orientation in Wallonia, and its status as the capital of the EU, is the major sticking point. There is also the question of what would happen to Belgium's tiny German-speaking region, as well as the fate of Belgium's monarchy, although surveys have shown that many younger Belgians believe a monarchy is unnecessary in the 21st century.

If Belgium did split, it's unlikely that Wallonia would join France, or that Flanders would join the Netherlands (though Dutch citizens overwhelmingly support Flanders becoming part of their country). Instead, one model for the future is that Flanders and Wallonia would each become independent, with Brussels becoming its own city-state, possibly administered by the EU. Certainly, the economic and legal unification provided by the EU makes it more viable than at any other time in modern history for such small nations to exist independently.

Still, the general sentiment in most quarters is that people don't want Belgium to split. Aside from personal attachment, a key pragmatic reason is that 'Belgian' has become a trademark, with considerable international standing as a byword for quality (such as 'Belgian chocolate' or 'Belgian beer'). Some feel this reputation may be diminished if Flanders and Wallonia split into separate countries, since these are lesser-known names internationally.

For the foreseeable future at least, it seems likely that Belgium will endure.

Local Life
Maison Antoine

Brussels can be divided into two kinds of people: those who swear by this chip shop, and those who pledge allegiance to the caravan on Place Flagey. **Maison Antoine's** (Place Jourdan; small chips from €2; ⏱11.30am-1am Sun-Thu, to 2am Fri & Sat; MSchuman) chips are twice-fried in beef fat, so they're twice as delicious; you'll see dignitaries, tourists and the odd celeb queuing for a coneful.

to the Paul-Henri Spaak section of the parliament. (☎02-284 34 57; www.europarl.europa.eu; Rue Wiertz 43; admission free; ⏱tours 10am & 3pm Mon-Thu, 10am Fri; 🚌38 direction Homborch, departs from next to Gare Centrale, to De Meeus on Rue du Luxembourg)

Square Marie-Louise   SQUARE

3 ◎ Map p112, B1

You can feed the ducks in this pretty tree-lined pond surrounded by greenery and a smattering of art nouveau architecture. (off Ave Palmerston; MMaelbeek)

Parc Léopold   PARK

4 ◎ Map p112, B3

Steep-sloping Parc Léopold was Brussels Zoo until 1880 and now forms an unexpectedly pleasant oasis, hidden away just behind the EU Parliament. (MSchuman)

Berlaymont Building

Berlaymont Building   BUILDING

5 ◎ Map p112, C2

The European Commission, the EU's sprawling bureaucracy, centres on the vast, four-winged Berlaymont building. Built in 1967, it's striking but by no means beautiful, despite a billion-euro rebuild between 1991 and 2004 that removed asbestos-tainted construction materials. Information panels dotted around the building give insight into the history of this neighbourhood and Brussels' international role. The building is not open to the public. (Rue de la Loi 200; MSchuman)

Eating

L'Atelier Européen   BELGIAN €€

6 Map p112, C2

Tucked down an alley and fronted
by a hedged courtyard, this former
wine warehouse has a pared-back
but sophisticated menu of meat and
fish dishes, such as sautéed veal and
grilled sea bass, with a couple (but
only a couple) of offerings for vegetar-
ians. Wine is given its due, with a
well-chosen list and monthly specials.
(02-734 91 40; www.atelier-euro.be; Rue
Franklin 28; mains €14-29; noon-2.30pm &
7-10.30pm Mon-Fri; MSchuman)

Stirwen   FRENCH €€€

7 Map p112, C4

This long-established Franco-
Belgian restaurant is popular with
a discerning EU crowd. The decor
is rather dark and conservative, but
the classic and traditional French
cooking is always reliable. (02-640
85 41; www.stirwen.be; Chaussée St-Pierre
15; mains €28-36; noon-midnight Mon-Fri;
MSchuman)

Au Bain Marie   ITALIAN €€

8 Map p112, C3

Despite the name, it's actually a
casual and welcoming Italian restaurant. Sit outside on the terrace in
summer. (02-280 48 88; Rue Breydel
46; mains from €13; noon-10pm Mon-Fri;
MSchuman)

Capoue   ICE CREAM €

9 Map p112, E3

Great ice cream in a dizzying variety
of flavours, including *speculoos*,
Belgium's trademark biscuit. It also
serves frozen yoghurt and snacks.

Top Tip

Art Nouveau in the EU Quarter

Private **Hôtel van Eetvelde** (Ave
Palmerston 2-4; MSchuman) can only
be accessed on an **ARAU tour**
(ARAU; 02-219 33 45; www.arau.org;
Blvd Adolphe Max 55; Apr–mid-Dec;
MDe Brouckère). While the outside
of this building is not Brussels'
most gripping, its interior is a Horta
masterpiece studded with exotic
timbers and sporting a central
glass dome infused with African-
inspired plant motifs. Its owner,
Baron Van Eetvelde, was at that
time Minister for the Congo and,
not coincidentally, the country's
highest-paid civil servant.

Narrow **Maison St-Cyr** (Sq
Ambiorix 11; closed; MSchuman)
has a classic 1903 facade that's
remarkable for its naturalistic
copper-framed window, filigree balconies and a circular upper portal.
It's crowned by a devil-may-care
topknot of extravagantly twisted
ironwork.

EU Parliament (p113)

(☎ 02-705 37 10; www.capoue.com; Ave des Celtes 36; ⏱ noon-10pm; Ⓜ Mérode)

Drinking

Café de l'Autobus BAR
10 🍷 Map p112, C4

This old-timers' bar is opposite Maison Antoine, the city's most famous *friture* (chip shop). The owners don't mind if you demolish a cone of *frites* while downing a beer or two. On Sunday it's a breather for vendors from the Place Jourdan food market. (☎ 02-230 63 16; Place Jourdan; Ⓜ Schuman)

Chez Bernard BAR
11 🍷 Map p112, C4

At this old-fashioned, classic Belgian bar, beer is most definitely the main attraction. You can buy your chips from Maison Antoine, opposite, and sit down to tuck into them with a drink Chez Bernard. (☎ 02-231 10 73; Place Jourdan 47; ⏱ 11am-midnight; Ⓜ Schuman)

Piola Libri BAR
12 🍷 Map p112, D1

Italian Eurocrats relax after work on sofas, at pavement tables or in the tiny triangle of back garden and enjoy free tapas-style snacks with chilled white wines at this convivial

Understand
'French' Fries

Just as the Brussels waffle actually originates from Ghent, French fries in fact hail from Belgium. The misnomer evolved during WWI in West Flanders, when English officers heard their Belgian counterparts speaking French while consuming fries and mistook their nationality (military orders were given in French, even to Dutch-only-speaking soldiers, with tragic consequences).

Fries here are made from Belgian- or Netherlands-grown *bintje* potatoes. They're hand-cut about 1cm thick – any smaller and they absorb too much oil and burn – and cooked first at a lower temperature then again at a higher temperature to become crispy on the outside while remaining soft inside. This double-cooking is what distinguished the Belgian chip from its flabbier counterparts elsewhere. Typically, *frites* are served in a paper cone and liberally smothered in a rich sauce. There are dozens of sauces including the classic, mayonnaise. If you're bewildered by the choice, take a chance with Andalouse, which is like very mildly spiced 1000-island dressing.

bookshop-*café*-bar. It has an eclectic program of readings and DJ nights. (📞 02-736 93 91; www.piolalibri.be; Rue Franklin 66; ⏱ noon-8pm Mon-Fri, to 6pm Sat, closed Aug; 📶; Ⓜ Schuman)

La Terrasse   PUB

13 🍺 Map p112, E3

Handy for the Cinquantenaire, this wood-panelled classic *café* (pub) has a tree-shaded terrace and makes an ideal refreshment stop after a hard day's museuming. Snacks, pancakes, ice creams, breakfasts (from €3.90) and decent pub meals are all available at various times. Try sampling the 'beer of the month'. (📞 02-732 28 51; www.brasserielaterrasse.be; Ave des Celtes 1; beers €2.40-4.50, mains €9.90-18; ⏱ 8am-midnight Mon-Sat, 10am-midnight Sun; Ⓜ Mérode)

Entertainment

Arcade du Cinquantenaire   CINEMA

14 ⭐ Map p112, D3

Ask the tourist office for the program of summertime drive-in movie screenings (with headphones available for nondrivers) under the Arcade du Cinquantenaire triumphal arch in the Parc du Cinquantenaire. (Parc du Cinquantenaire; Ⓜ Mérode)

Shopping

Crush Wine   DRINK

15 🔒 Map p112, A3

Wondrous cellar stocking over 190 Australian wines (the most comprehensive

Parc Léopold (p115)

selection in Europe). Look out for rare drops from Tasmania and deliberate over dozens of Margaret River reds. There are daily tastings and tapas and regular wine events; call ahead for the schedule of Saturday openings. (📞02-502 66 97; www.crushwine.be; Rue Caroly 39; ⏱11am-7pm Mon-Fri plus 1 Sat per month; Ⓜ Trône)

Place Jourdan Market
MARKET

16 🔒 Map p112, C4

Place Jourdan hosts a small Sunday-morning market selling food and clothes. (Place Jourdan; ⏱7am-2pm Sun; Ⓜ Schuman)

Top Sights
Musée Horta

Getting There

🚌 92 runs from Place Louise (15 minutes; every 15 minutes).

The exterior doesn't give much away, but Victor Horta's former home (designed and built 1898–1901) is an art nouveau jewel. Bathed in warm colours, the ground-floor living areas incorporate gleaming floor-to-ceiling tiling, while upstairs you can see Horta's personalised touches in the small, intimate rooms. The lower level offers an overview of his work, including a model of his magnificent Maison du Peuple, which tragically met with the wrecking ball.

Art-nouveau stairwell

Don't Miss

Stairwell
The stairwell is the structural triumph of the house – follow the playful knots and curlicues of the banister, which become more exuberant as you ascend, ending at a tangle of swirls and glass lamps at the skylight, glazed with plain and citrus-coloured glass.

Dining Room
Floor mosaics, glittering stained glass, and ceramic brick walls reflect the light in this superbly harmonious room, rich with swirling American ash furniture, glowing brass and a pink-and-orange colour scheme. The room opens into a salon, with glass doors creating a sense of flow into the garden beyond.

Bedrooms
There is more honey-coloured American ash in Horta's bedroom, where a closet reveals a discrete and handy urinal. Horta's daughter's room has a pretty winter garden, while you can only envy people who were invited to stay in the guest bedroom at the top of the house.

Exterior
As is typical of Horta's work, the exterior is relatively austere, though nice to contemplate once you've been inside – look out for the dragonfly-shaped railing of the guestroom window and the aesthetic/industrial metal balcony.

📞 02-543 04 90

www.hortamuseum.be

Rue Américaine 25

adult/child €8/4

🕑 2-5.30pm Tue-Sun

Ⓜ Horta, 🚌 91, 92

☑ Top Tips

▶ There's an excellent museum guide (€10).

▶ Visits are limited to 45 people – arrive early to avoid queuing.

▶ Guided tours in English are available on request.

▶ See the house with an expert guide on an **ARAU** (📞 02-219 33 45; www.arau. org; 3hr; €19) bus tour.

▶ Discover art nouveau Brussels on foot (p128).

✕ Take a Break

Have a glass of wine and a cheese platter at stylish **Oeno tk** (📞 02-534 64 34; 86 Rue Africains, Saint-Gille; 🕑 11am-8pm Mon & Tue, to 10.30pm Wed-Sat).

Local Life
A Stroll in the Marolles

Getting There

Take the glass elevator from Place Poelaert, in front of the Palais de Justice down the steep hill to the Marolles.

Ⓜ Gare du Midi and Porte de Hal are the handiest metro stations for the district.

Brussels' partially gentrified working-class area, the Marolles, is known for its colourful dialect and down-to-earth watering holes. To appreciate the area's roots, head to Place du Jeu-de-Balle or pop into a neighbourhood bar. Crumbling brick chimneys are another remnant of the area's industrial past. Visit on Sunday for the Gare du Midi market (though the brewery will be closed) – to take in morning Mass at the church visit these sights in a different order!

❶ Taste Some Brews

If you're in the area from Monday to Saturday, start your tour at **Museé Bruxellois de la Gueuze** (📞02-521 49 28; www.cantillon.be; Rue Gheude 56; admission €7; ⏰9am-5pm Mon-Fri, 10am-5pm Sat; Ⓜ Clemenceau), which gives you behind-the-scenes insight into the production of these unique lambic beers. And, of course, you get to taste some, too.

❷ Wander Gare du Midi Market

If you're visiting on a Sunday, head to the Gare du Midi **market** (Gare du Midi; ⏰6am-1pm Sun; Ⓜ Gare du Midi), said to be the biggest in Europe. This sprawl of colourful stalls next to the railway lines has an international flavour, with exotic North African and Mediterranean spices, cheeses, meats, clothing and leather goods.

❸ Jeu-de-Balle Flea Market

The quintessential Marolles experience is haggling at this chaotic **flea market** (Place du Jeu-de-Balle; ⏰7am-2pm; Ⓜ Porte de Hal, 🚊Lemonnier). Weekends see it at its liveliest, but for the best bargains, head here early morning midweek. Stop for a coffee at Le Marsellais on the northeast corner of the square: 55 varieties of pastis are served here.

❹ Walk up Rue des Renard

This narrow street exemplifies how the area is changing – on the left heading uphill are trendy vintage and retro shops, on the right cottages and traditional restaurants. At the top you'll often find a vestige of the old Marolles: a cart selling little pots of snails.

❺ View Horta's Jardin d'Enfants

This lovely Horta **building** (Rue St-Ghislain 40; Ⓜ Porte de Hal) is a school, so you'll only be able to view it from the outside. Look for sinuous plant motifs, a playful tower, and stripes of grey and pale stone.

❻ Check out the Brueghel House

There is a museum in this step-gabled **house** (📞02-513 89 40; Rue Haute 132) where Pieter Brueghel the Elder lived and died, but it's only open by reservation; phone ahead or check with the tourist office for details.

❼ See St-Jeanne-et-Étienne aux Minimes

The area's church is a huge, sooty and weather-beaten baroque structure, completed in 1715. If you visit on Sunday at 11.30am you can go to Mass – the acoustics of the ribbed cupola are very good, and Mass features either Gregorian chants or Bach cantatas.

❽ Dine at L'Idiot du Village

Booking ahead is essential to secure a table at the colourful **L'Idiot du Village** (📞02-502 55 82; www.lidiotduvillage. be; Rue Notre Seigneur 19; mains around €30; ⏰noon-2pm & 7.30-11pm Mon-Fri; Ⓜ Louise), secluded on a little side street north of the Place du Jeu-de-Balle. The Belgian dishes are rich and aromatic (lots of herbs) and portions are generous.

Local Life
Shopping in Ste-Catherine

Ste-Catherine is a byword for what's hippest and happening right now in the capital. The main drag, Rue Antoine Dansaert, forms the focal point for Brussels' rapidly rising fashion scene, featuring avant-garde home-grown designers, while Rue de Flandre and Rue Léon Lepage host smaller and quirkier boutiques. Window shop or drop some cash, and hang out in the hip neighbourhood *cafés* (pubs).

Getting There

🚇The nearest premetro station is Bourse, but it'll take you no more than 15 minutes to walk here from the Grand Place.

Ⓜ The nearest metro station is Ste-Catherine.

❶ Vintage Treasures at Gabriele

For amazing vintage finds try eccentric, elegant **Gabriele** (☎02-512 67 43; gabrielevintage.com; Rue des Chartreux 27; ⏱1-7pm Mon & Tue, 11am-7pm Wed-Sat; 🚇Bourse). There's a gorgeous jumble of cocktail dresses, hats, Chinese shawls and accessories; only original clothes from the '20s to the '80s are stocked.

❷ Books at Passa Porta

This stylish **bookshop** (www.passaporta. be; Rue Antoine Dansaert 46; ⏱11am-7pm Tue-Sat, noon-6pm Sun; 🚇Bourse) located down an alley has a small but classy English-language section. Look out for the leaflet listing literary events, many of which are hosted in English and offer a great chance to mingle with locals.

❸ Designer Garb at Stijl

Stijl (www.stijl.be; Rue Antoine Dansaert 74; 🚇Ste-Catherine) is well stocked with Antwerp Six classic designer-wear, but also features up-to-the-minute designers including Haider Ackermann, Gustavo Lins and Raf Simons. It's a hip place but not unduly daunting to enter and, unlike many such boutiques, prices are clearly labelled. Has fashion for men and women.

❹ Fashion at Just in Case

Poetic and feminine garments with vintage-style shapes. The beautiful clothes at **Just in Case** (justincase.be; Rue Léon Lepage 63; ⏱11am-7pm Tue-Sat; 🚇Ste-Catherine) are arranged by colour: electric blue, coral and orange.

❺ Bargains at Outlet Privejoke

Casual fashion for men and women without a hefty price tag at this small **outlet store** (Rue Léon Lepage 30; ⏱2-7pm Wed-Sun; 🚇Ste-Catherine). Good for functional jackets and separates.

❻ Drink at Au Laboureur

Sample old Brussels when you need some refreshment: this characterful corner **bar** (Rue de Flandre 108; beer €1.60; ⏱9.30am-10pm; 🚇Ste-Catherine) is a great beer-stop and a reminder of the area's past.

❼ Quirky Fashion at Lowi

Browse idiosyncratic fashion and accessories at **Lowi** (www.lowi.be; Rue de Flandre 124; ⏱11am-6.30pm Tue-Sat; 🚇Ste-Catherine), including covetable ceramic and porcelain jewellery.

❽ Cooking Heaven at Pimpinelle

This cute **boutique** (www.pimpinelle.be; Rue de Flandre 57; ⏱11am-6.30pm Thu-Sat, closed Aug; 🚇Ste-Catherine) sells pale ceramics and utilitarian tin plates, plus cake tins, pots and pans, and scales. It also runs cookery workshops in the attractively tiled back room.

❾ Crafty Micro Marché

Round off your shopping with something different: the alternative and affordable handmade crafts at boho **Micro Marché** (www.micromarche.com; Quai à la Houille 9; ⏱4-9pm Fri, 11am-7pm Sat & Sun; 🚇Ste-Catherine). The industrial courtyard has been converted into a performance and exhibition space, plus there's a travellers' *café* (pub), all of which makes it a bit of a hub in the area.

The Best of
Bruges & Brussels

Bruges & Brussels' Best Walks

Bruges & Brussels' Best...

Restaurants on the Markt (p24), Bruges
GONZALO AZUMENDI/GETTY IMAGES ©

Best Walks
Art Nouveau Brussels

🏃 The Walk

Art nouveau is the signature architectural style of Brussels, and its most significant exponent was Victor Horta (1861–1947), an architectural chameleon mostly remembered for daring, light-suffused buildings using trademark elements of wrought iron and glass. His celebrated Maison du Peuple was torn down in 1965, but surviving masterpieces can be explored on this route, along with some lovely buildings by his contemporaries. Only Musée Horta is open to the public – to see some interiors take one of ARAU's excellent tours (p121).

Start Porte de Hal; **M** Porte de Hal

Finish Ave Louise

Length 3km; two hours

🍴 Take a Break

End your walk with a drink at superhip **Café Belga** (📞 02-640 35 08; www.cafebelga.be; Place Flagey 18; 🕗 8am-2am Sun-Thu, to 3am Fri & Sat; 🚊 81, 82).

MARTIN MOOS/GETTY IMAGES ©

Art nouveau detailing at Hôtel Solvay, Brussels

❶ La Porteuse d'Eau

Head down Chaussée de Waterloo from the fairy-tale Porte de Hal, and turn right onto Ave Jean Volders. At No 48 you can have a coffee at classic art nouveau La Porteuse d'Eau, featuring spectacular stained glass and ornate wooden booths.

❷ Hôtel Winssinger

The Hôtel Winssinger is a sober Horta building that, typically, does not call attention to itself. Look for the characteristic pale stone, as well as the use of metal around the windows and the dainty swirling balconies.

❸ Musée Victor Horta

You may want to visit **Horta's house** (p121) separately to give yourself plenty of time. But do pause to admire the exterior, characteristically simple but featuring a playful motif in the dragonfly terrace. The interior is flooded with light from above and alive with swirling lines.

4 Les Hiboux & Hôtel Hannon

Ave Brugmann brings you to two delightful adjoining art nouveau buildings: Édouard Pelseneer's red-brick Les Hiboux, surmounted by two Gothic owls, and Jules Brunfaut's Hôtel Hannon, graced by stone friezes and stained glass.

5 Maison & Atelier Dubois

Close by at No 80 is another Horta building, commissioned by his friend, designer Fernand Dubois. It's now the Cuban embassy, but you can see from the outside how the large windows must have flooded the studio with light.

6 Hankar Studio

Paul Hankar's buildings on Rue Defacqz are externally much more exuberant constructs than Horta's. Rue Defacqz 71 is an 1893 house designed by Hankar (1859–1901) as his own studio.

7 Hôtel Tassel

Rue Paul-Émile Janson 6 is the site of Horta's first truly art nouveau house, the 1893 Hôtel Tassel. It's a masterwork. Horta designed the mosaics, stained glass, woodwork, even the door handles.

8 Hôtel Solvay

At No 224 on grandiose Avenue Louise you'll find Horta designed Hôtel Solvay, considered one of his masterpieces. Again, he designed every element of the house, incorporating luxurious materials such as tropical wood, bronze and onyx, though the exterior is plain. It's open only to ARAU tours.

Best Walks
Bruges' Parks & Canals

🏃 The Walk

This circular walk takes you from the heart of Bruges to some of its most charming green spaces: the Koningin Astridpark with its little bandstand, the elongated park along Gentpoortvest, spacious Minnewater and the attractive courtyard of the *begijnhof*. Beyond this point you circle back to the more touristy environs of the Vismarkt. An excellent patisserie en route provides perfect picnic fodder.

Start Vismarkt

Finish Vismarkt

Length 3km; two hours

🍴 Take a Break

This route features the splendid little **Patisserie Schaeverbeke** (☎050 33 31 82; Schaarstraat 2), piled with creamy fruity cakes, croissants and fresh fragrant bread. Stock up here for a picnic in the Minnewater; you can also buy fresh fruit at the greengrocer across the road.

Koningin Astridpark, Bruges

MICHAELUTECH/GETTY IMAGES ©

❶ Vismarkt

The handsome colonnaded 1821 **fish market** (p42) is still open for business most days. Fishmongers have been selling their North Sea produce for centuries, though these days only a few vendors set up on the cold stone slabs. Join locals buying snacks such as *maatjes* (herring fillets). Several seafood restaurants here back onto pretty Huidenvettersplein, where archetypal Bruges buildings, including the old tanners' guildhall, are located.

❷ Koningin Astridpark

This attractive park was named for the Swedish wife of King Léopold of Belgium – you can see her bust in the corner of the park, as well as a bandstand. Exit the park by the Gothic revival Magdalen Church; scrumptious **Patisserie Schaeverbeke** is at Schaarstraat 2.

❸ Gentpoort

Gentpoort is one of the town's four medieval gateways. From here, a pleasant footpath leads through the greenery along the water's edge.

4 Minnewater Park

Minnewater Park is a scenic green space with orderly flower beds and secluded paths. It's hard to believe that the serene lake here, now known to Bruges-dwellers as the 'Lake of Love', was once the inner harbour of the city where exotic cargoes of wool, wine, spices and silks were unloaded.

5 Wijngaardplein

Wijngaardplein, a touristy but still irresistible square, is ringed by *cafés* (pubs) and features a horse-head fountain where the city's carriage horses are watered. The *cafés* here are a little on the pricey side, but the views are refreshing.

6 Begijnhof

Over the little arched bridge from the square, the 13th-century **begijnhof** (p50) is one of the delights of Bruges, its whitewashed buildings encircling a garden with tall trees and swaths of daffodils in spring. It's

well worth visiting **'t Begijnhuisje** (p51), the house museum here, as well as the church. From the *begijnhof,* cross the water and head up Wijngaard-straat to turn left onto Katelijnestraat.

Bear right onto Gruuthusestraat (which becomes Dijver) and head back to the Vis-markt.

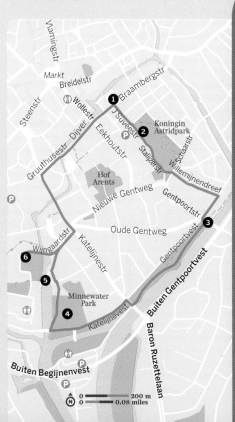

Best Walks
Back Streets of Western Bruges

🏃 The Walk

One of the chief pleasures of Bruges is to simply wander with no agenda. This short walk takes you from the Markt to the west of the city in a little loop, taking in historic churches, Renaissance mansions and almshouses. There are no show-stopping sights, but you'll find fewer tourists and more tranquillity as soon as you head even a short distance away from the centre.

Start Markt

Finish Markt

Length 2.5km; 1½ to two hours

🍴 Take a Break

Just off Zuidzandstraat is tucked-way Dweerstraat, where the candlelit **Gran Kaffe De Passage** (p37) bistro serves hearty and filling Belgian food at bargain prices.

Speelmansrei, Bruges

❶ Markt

The walk starts at the **Markt** (p24), the heart of Bruges, with its fantastical neo-Gothic buildings and the tall Belfort tower looming above. From the square, take the street that leads to the southwest: Steenstraat, with its fine 17th-century facades.

❷ Simon Stevinplein

Here you can detour into the attractive square on the right-hand side, named for 16th-century Bruges mathematician and physician Simon Stevin, to sample the wares at the **Chocolate Line** (p60), run by Dominique Persoone, the city's most outrageous and innovative chocolatier. The surprising flavours include Cuban cigar and wasabi.

❸ Zuidzandstraat

Zuidzandstraat leads down to 't Zand. Cross the square to bear left onto Boeveriestraat. Or you can detour to another square, Beursplein, where live chickens, rabbits, food and flowers are sold at the market on Saturday mornings.

④ Boerievest

Here the route approaches the water, where you'll see the scenic old **Waterhuis**. Horses operated a wheel here to pull water out of the canal, which was then used to supply wells and breweries. Turn right to take the path through the stretch of parkland. Soon you come to **Smedenpoort**, a 14th-century city gate.

⑤ Smedenstraat

Turn right back in the direction of the city centre up Smedenstraat. A detour here up Kreupelenstraat or Kammakersstraat takes you to some typical Bruges almshouses.

⑥ Speelmansrei

Speelmansrei curves to the left, following the left bank of the canal for a stretch. Cross the canal and turn left onto Moerstraat, then right onto Ontvangersstraat. Head down and turn

left onto bustling Noordzanstraat.

⑦ Eiermarkt

A final detour is to peek at little Muntplein off to the left, where locals gather to eat ice cream from **Da Vinci** (p37). Then you join the attractive *café*-encircled mini square of Eiermarkt, before returning to spacious Markt.

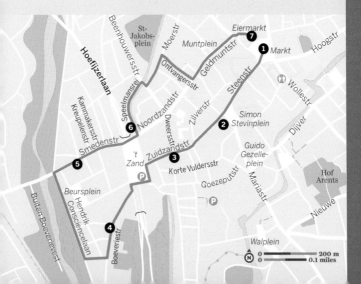

Best
Eating

Bring a healthy appetite with you – restaurants in Brussels and Bruges dish up a seemingly endless procession of delicious fare. What's more, Belgium boasts more Michelin stars per capita than anywhere in Europe. Many *cafés* (bars and pubs) also serve hearty meals.

LONELY PLANET/GETTY IMAGES ©

What to Eat

Breakfast in Flanders is a hearty affair of cured meats, cheeses, cereals and so on. At lunchtime many restaurants offer a dish of the day (*dagschotel* in Dutch; *plat du jour* in French). Also watch for a 'menu of the day' (*dagmenu; menu du jour*). These set menus comprise three or more courses and work out cheaper than ordering individual courses à la carte. Some kitchens open as early as 6pm for dinner, but most don't get busy until at least a couple of hours later.

Mussels & Frites

If Belgium has a national dish, it is mussels (*mosselen* in Dutch; *moules* in French). Forget about using a fork to scoop out these much-loved molluscs; use an empty shell as a pincher to prise them out. Fries (*frietenin; frites*) are even more ubiquitous. Not only do they accompany mussels (and virtually any other dish), but they are easily Belgium's favourite snack.

Meat Lovers

Those of a delicate disposition, beware: Belgians' idea of *saignant* (rare) meat drips with blood; *à point* (medium) is what other nationalities consider rare, and *bien cuit* is the closest you'll get to well done (these French terms are also used by Dutch speakers). 'Blue' steaks will barely have bounced off the grill.

☑ Top Tips

Best Belgian eats:

▶ *Bloedworst* (pig's blood black pudding, with apple sauce)

▶ *Breugel Kop* (beef and tongue set in gelatine)

▶ *Filet américain* (minced beef served raw)

▶ *Konijnmet pruimen* (tender rabbit in prune sauce)

▶ *Paar de filet/steack de cheval* (horse steak)

▶ *Palingin 'groen/ anguilles-au-vert* (eel in spinach sauce)

▶ *Stoemp* (mashed potato topped with a sausage)

Best for Belgian Food, Brussels

Brasserie de la Roue d'Or Sample suckling pig and steak. (p77)

Maison Antoine Allegedly the finest chips in town. (p115)

Dandoy The best place to sample Brussels' biscuits. (p76; pictured, left)

Mokafé Authentic icing-sugar-sprinkled waffles. (p74)

Best for Belgian Food, Bruges

Den Dyjver Excellent food cooked in Belgian beer. (p56)

In 't Nieuwe Museum Backstreet joint serving eel, steaks and casseroles. (p38)

Christophe Flemish fare, including many variations of steak. (p57)

Restobières Belgian-beer-themed food. (p100)

Best for Haute Cuisine, Brussels

L'Ogenblik Delightful old-town bistro. (p76)

La Maison du Cygne Fine dining on the Grand Place. (p78)

Stirwen Posh eating in the EU district. (p116)

Sea Grill The town's best seafood in a fancy hotel restaurant. (p78)

L'Atelier Européen Secluded and smart restaurant for the Euro set. (p116)

Best for Haute Cuisine, Bruges

De Karmeliet Complex and elegant food in a Michelin-starred restaurant. (p36)

Den Gouden Harynck Swish and sophisticated, in a gorgeous old building. (p56)

Best Ethnic Restaurants

Ryad Moroccan tagines, Indian curries and a Berber tea lounge in Bruges. (p38)

Kokob Ethopian food in Brussels, served in a welcoming atmosphere. (p77)

Best for Seafood, Bruges

Den Gouden Karpel By the fish market, serving crab, shrimps and oysters. (p36)

De Stove Fish dishes, with everything caught daily. (p35)

Chagall Eel and mussels are on the menu in this cosy place. (p36)

Best for Escaping the Crowds, Bruges

De Belegde Boterham Smart lunch spot patronised by locals. (p29)

L'Estaminet Friendly bistro just off the beaten track by the Koningen park. (p29)

De Windmolen Cute cafe-bar in the shadow of the St-Anna windmills. (p31)

De Stoepa Backstreet bistro with a tranquil terrace garden. (p56)

Best
Drinking & Nightlife

You'll encounter a bewildering choice of Belgian beers and *jenevers* (gin) at just about every drinking establishment, but the best places to try these are specialist '*jenever cafés*' and 'beer pubs'. In bars and clubs, jazz is the style of live music you'll encounter most often. Look out for flyers in music shops, streetwear boutiques, bars and *cafés* about DJ nights, club fixtures and one-off parties.

Drinking Culture

At specialised drinking establishments, you'll be handed a thick menu detailing hundreds of varieties. Wading through the menus is a Herculean feat: ask the staff for the flavours and characteristics you have in mind and be guided by them. Drinking establishments usually open around 10am; closing hours aren't restricted by law but simply depend on how busy it is on the night.

Where to Drink

Cafés always serve alcohol and some, though not all, also serve food. Places that do are sometimes classified as an *eetcafé* (eating cafe) or a *grand café* (a larger, more elegant version of an *eetcafé*), and it's fine to just stop in for a drink even if you're not dining. You can also just pop in for a drink at a brasserie or bistro, although these are chiefly eateries. Anywhere that labels itself a bar generally only serves drinks. Likewise, a *herberg* (Dutch for 'tavern') is primarily a drinking spot. One of the most atmospheric *cafés* for drinking is the traditional *bruin café* ('brown cafe', sometimes called a *bruine kroeg*). So named for their wood panelling, interspersed with oversize mirrors, these small, cosy, old-fashioned pubs are prime places for mixing with locals.

WIBOWO RUSLI/GETTY IMAGES ©

☑ Top Tips

▶ Drinking with locals, you'll notice that everyone buys rounds (all but 'Bob' – the name Belgians give to a designated driver, thanks to a hugely successful campaign against drink-driving).

▶ You'll also notice locals ordering beers using a bizarre sign language.

▶ Remember to say 'Cheers!' – in Dutch, *schol* (or *gezondheid* – 'to your health'), and in French, *santé!*

Rue des Bouchers (p75), Brussels

Best Specialist Beer Pubs, Brussels

À la Mort Subite Try its speciality *gueuze* (lambic beer). (p79)

Moeder Lambic Fontainas Hip bar serving artisanal beers. (p82)

La Fleur en Papier Doré Old-style pub, once frequented by Magritte. (p79)

Best Specialist Beer Pubs, Bruges

't Brugs Beertje Cosy and full of character, with a huge range of brews. (p58)

De Garre Brace your tastebuds for 11% Garre beer. (p40)

't Poatersgat Cellar bar with umpteen Trappist beers on offer. (p39)

Herberg Vlissinghe Simply unmissable: the oldest bar in the city. (p39)

Cambrinus Historic beer bar in a 17th-century gabled building. (p40)

Best Live Music Bars, Brussels

Le Cercle des Voyageurs Live jazz plus good food and wine. (p76)

Music Village Long-established classy jazz bar. (p83)

Art Base Small venue for serious music lovers. (p84)

Best Live Music Bars, Bruges

Du Phare Blues and jazz venue at the north end of town. (p42)

Retsin's Lucifernum Live Latin music in extraordinary environs. (p41)

Est Wijnbar Sunday-night jazz in a cute little wine bar. (p38)

Best
Entertainment

Considering it was an opera performance that sparked the revolution for Belgian independence, it's not surprising the performing arts are celebrated across the country. Brussels boasts dozens of superb venues, while Bruges has its own state-of-the-art venue, the Concertgebouw. There are also some charming traditional puppet theatres, notably the Théâtre Royal de Toone.

Belgian Cinema

The Belgian love of cinema seems easily explained by two things: the fact that nightlife doesn't start until late, and the climate. The country brims with cinemas, though the industry itself is underfunded compared with other art forms.

An average of just two mainstream Belgian films are released per year, in addition to smaller, lower-budget independent releases. But Belgian directors are internationally renowned, chief among them brothers Luc and Jean-Pierre Dardenne: their recent film, *The Kid with a Bike,* won the Grand Prix at Cannes Film Festival in 2011, while harrowing *Rosetta* (1999) and the rather more uplifting *L'Enfant* (2005) were both awarded the Palme d'Or. Bruges itself also starred memorably in 2008's hilarious action-comedy *In Bruges,* in which Colin Farrell and Brendan Gleeson play hitmen ordered by their boss (Ralph Fiennes) to hide out in the city during the pre-Christmas frenzy.

Local Stars

Unlike its directors, Belgium's film stars generally aren't well known outside their own country, the exception being Brussels' action-hero Jean-Claude Van Damme. Local stars include Vincent Grass, Natacha Amal and Matthias Schoenaerts.

☑ Top Tip

▶ There's no need to seek out cinema chains in the capital: the most character-ful movie houses are small and independent, tucked away in elegant glassed galleries and down side streets.

Best for Theatre, Music & Dance, Brussels

BOZAR Magnificent Horta-designed concert hall. (p103)

Théâtre du Vaudeville Theatre, concerts and cabaret. (p85)

Théâtre Royal de la Monnaie Hear a concert where Belgian's revolution began. (p85; pictured above right)

Théâtre Royal de la Monnaie (p85), Brussels

AB Best for pop and rock acts. (p85)

Théâtre National Gleaming French-language theatre. (p86)

Cirque Royal Big-name bands, concerts and dance. (p103)

Recyclart Alternative and grafitti-covered arts venue. (p96; pictured, above left)

Best for Theatre, Music & Dance, Bruges

Koninklijke Stadsschouwburg A grand venue for classical music, dance and theatre. (p41)

Concertgebouw This modern concert hall shows top-drawer music and dance. (p58)

Cactus Muziekcentrum World and modern music, plus its own music festival. (p58)

Best Cinemas, Brussels

Actor's Studio Hunt the alleys for this art-house gem. (p85)

Cinéma Galeries Tucked away in the Galeries St-Hubert. (p83)

Cinematek Art-house classics and silent films with live accompaniment. (p103)

Best Belgian Film Festivals

Anima, Brussels & Ghent (www.animatv.be) In February, Brussels' animated-film festival attracts top-quality shorts and features.

Cinema Novo Film Festival, Bruges (www.cinemanovo.be) In March, independent films from Asia, Africa and Latin America are screened in Bruges.

Best
Gay & Lesbian

Brussels is Belgium's magnet for gay and lesbian visitors. The legendary event is the city's monthly La Démence club night (www.lademence.com), when bold and beautiful boys from all over Europe come to kick up their heels. The Festival du Film Gay & Lesbien de Bruxelles (www.fglb.org) takes place in late January, while the Belgian Gay & Lesbian Pride parade hits the streets in May. In general, the attitude to gay visitors is relaxed and accepting; in terms of legislation, Belguim is progressive about rights for same-sex couples.

MICHAEL LUHRENBERG/GETTY IMAGES ©

The Scene

Brussels' gay and lesbian scene is concentrated around Rue du Marché au Charbon, Rue des Pierres and Rue de la Fourche in the heart of the city. Pick up the bimonthly booklet *Zizo* (in Dutch but easily navigable for nonspeakers), published by Holebifoon (www.holebifoon.be), which lists dozens of venues throughout the country. Bruges' tourist office keeps an updated list of gay-friendly establishments.

☑ **Top Tip**

▶ After La Démence, many revellers kick on at the **Royal Windsor Hotel** (📞02 505 55 55; www.royal-windsorbrussels.com; Rue Duquesnoy 5).

Gay-friendly Venues, Brussels

Chez Maman (📞02-502 86 96; www.chezmaman. be; Rue des Grands Carmes 12; admission free; ⏰from 10pm Fri & Sat; 🚊Anneessens) Features the capital's most beloved transvestite show.

Fontainas Bar (📞02-503 31 12; Rue du Marché au

Charbon 91; ⏰10am-late Mon-Fri, 11am-late Sat & Sun; 🚊Bourse) Ultratrendy bar with ripped black-vinyl seats, '60s tables and light fittings, and cracked tiles. The party cranks up again come nightfall. (p81)

Le Belgica (www.lebelgica. be; Rue du Marché au Charbon 32; ⏰10pm-3am Thu-Sun;

🚊Bourse) DJs transform what looks like a 1920s traditional brown cafe into one of Brussels' most popular gay music pubs.

Fuse (www.fuse.be; Rue Blaes 208; cover €5-12; ⏰11pm-7am Sat; Ⓜ Porte de Hal) Once a month it hosts epic gay night La Démence.

Le Club (45 Rue des Pierres; ⏰5pm-late; 🚊Bourse) Hosts transvestite nights and club nights.

Best
Markets

The full spectrum of markets set up regularly in Bruges and Brussels – from elegant antiques markets and fairs trading rare china, crystal and furniture to flea markets spilling over with *brocante* (bric-a-brac) and secondhand treasures, including dog-eared comics, CDs and old vinyl records, plus new and vintage clothing. There are also rainbowlike food markets, where you can pick up the ingredients for the perfect picnic.

STUART BLACK/GETTY IMAGES ©

Market Nosh

Any time of year, the street fare sold from caravans parked at the markets is a treat: try steaming waffles that tickle your nose with icing sugar and cones full of mayonnaise-slathered fries.

Christmas Markets

Christmas season brings the most magical markets of all, when the cities' ancient squares fill with stalls selling handcrafted toys, nutcrackers, a dazzling array of ornaments and warming mugs of sweet mulled wine. Winter wonderlands of ice sculptures and outdoor skating rinks are erected most years (both generally take place throughout the month of December). Tourist offices can advise as to the markets' venues, but you can't go wrong by just following the crowds.

Best Markets, Brussels

Gare du Midi Market Piled with North African and Mediterranean goodies. (p123)

Place du Jeu-de-Balle Flea Market A favourite with local shoppers – sharpen your elbows for the daily give away of unsold stock. (p123)

Sablon Antiques Market Mosey around for treasures at this weekend market. (p104)

Grand Place Hosts a flower market three times a week on Monday, Wednesday and Friday mornings. (p66)

Place Jourdan Market Sunday market for food and clothes. (p119)

Best Markets, Bruges

Markt Historic Wednesday market ringed by stunning buildings. (p24; pictured)

Vismarkt The city's old fish market still purveys seafood and crafts. (p42)

Best
Shops

Beer and chocolate top most shopping lists for visitors to Brussels and Bruges, and the cities have an astonishing array of both. Other unique suitcase-stuffers include handmade lace, designer fashions, classic comics, diamonds and quality antiques. Bargain hunters should visit during the two annual sales periods – the first week in January, and the first week of July.

Buying Chocolate

Glinting light-brown, dark-brown and creamy-white coated squares, oblongs, balls and cups, embossed gold stamps and elaborate swirls, and wrapped in shimmering tinfoil or twisted inside cellophane. Yes, even shopping for chocolate is an art in Belgium – and it would want to be, with premium chocolates reaching €120 per kilogram. A turning point for Belgian chocolate came in 1912, when pralines (filled chocolates) were created in Brussels. Today these are undergoing another evolution at the hands of Belgium's mould-breaking chocolatiers, whose fusion pralines incorporate flavours such as Havana cigar, cauliflower, green pea, chilli and wasabi.

Outlets

In addition to the rarefied showrooms of top chocolatiers there are also numerous luxury chains. Popular local manufacturers include Leonidas, the original praline creator Neuhaus and Galler, which also offers its superb pralines (such as fresh pistachio-filled white chocolate) in chocolate-bar form.

GRANT FAINT/GETTY IMAGES ©

☑ Top Tip

▶ You'll find many top chain brands in supermarkets for a fraction of the price you pay at the boutiques. Temptation prevails right up until leaving the country – Brussels International Airport is the biggest chocolate-selling point in the world.

Best for Chocolate, Brussels

Mary Long-established speciality praline maker. (p104)

Pierre Marcolini High-profile designer chocolates. (p103)

Neuhaus Brussels' original chocolatier in the Galerie de la Reine. (p86)

De Biertempel (p86), Brussels

Laurent Gerbaud Attractive handmade chocs in original flavours. (p100)

Best for Fine Food, Chocolate & Beer, Bruges

Bacchus Cornelius Sells a fantastic variety of beers and *jenevers*. (p29)

Diksmuids Boterhuis Picturesque grocer selling fine meats and cheeses. (p29)

2-Be Belgian specialities, including chocolates, *jenevers* and beers. (p43)

Chocolate Line Sells delicious handmade and experimental chocolates. (p60)

Best Fashion, Bruges

L'Heroine An oasis of designer cool in Bruges. (p29)

Madam Mim Second-hand garments plus some handmade with vintage fabrics. (p29)

Olivier Strelli Colourful and sophisticated fashion for men and women. (p43)

Best Covered Arcades, Brussels

Galeries St-Hubert Follow in the shopping footsteps of Victor Hugo. (p75)

Passage du Nord Pretty arcade with an oyster bar and chocolate shop. (p87)

Best Speciality Shops, Brussels

Boutique Tintin The best of Hergé's boy reporter. (p86)

De Biertempel Piled to the ceiling with speciality beers. (p86; pictured above)

Best Speciality Shops, Bruges

't Apostelientje Wonderful handmade and vintage lace. (p31)

Rombaux Beautiful family-run music shop well worth a browse. (p43)

De Striep A wonderfully comprehensive stock of comic books. (p61)

♥ Best Museums & Galleries

RENATA SEDMAKOVA/SHUTTERSTOCK ©

Brussels and Bruges have a rich artistic tradition stretching back centuries; in true Belgian style, you'll also find irreverent sculptures and comic murals on display. The art movement that really captured Belgium's sense of the absurd was surrealism, and leading the charge was René Magritte, whose man in a bowler hat has become a national emblem.

Belgian Art

The distinction between Dutch and Flemish painters didn't come about until the late-16th century. However, the artists who were commissioned in the 15th century by nobility to record their life, times and religion, and would go on to influence the direction of European art, are today known as the Flemish Primitives. The 16th century saw Flemish painter Pieter Brueghel the Elder and his two sons, Pieter the Younger and Jan, make their mark on the artistic landscape. Perhaps Belgium's most renowned painter, though, was Pieter Paul Rubens (1577–1640). Born in Germany, Rubens returned to his parents' home town of Antwerp and utilised both Flemish and Italian styles to create his seminal religious works and voluptuous 'Rubenesque' nudes.

Contemporary Art

Belgium has a powerful contemporary art scene. Look out for works by Panamarenko, whose bizarre sculptures and paintings fuse authentic and imaginary flying contraptions; Jan Fabre, famed for his Bic-art (ballpoint drawings); powerful politically themed paintings by Luc Tuymans; and Eddy Stevens, who combines elements of Rubens' lustrous realism with surrealist twists.

Best for Flemish Primitives

Musées Royaux des Beaux-Arts A wonderful Brussels showcase of the work of Van der Weyden and co. (p90; pictured above)

Groeningemuseum Bruges museum with sublime works by the masters of refined oil-painting. (p46)

Memlingmuseum (Bruges) Six jewel-bright works by the great Hans Memling. (p48)

Best for Decorative Arts, Brussels

Musées Royaux des Beaux-Arts Art nouveau and art deco treasures. (p90)

Musée Horta Horta's own wonderfully designed home. (p121)

Lace at Musée du Costume et de la Dentelle (p72), Brussels

Best Speciality Museums, Brussels

Musée du Costume et de la Dentelle Stunning lace-bedecked clothes. (p72; pictured above)

Musée des Instruments de Musique Fascinating and unusual music museum. (p92)

Musée Magritte Surrealist fun: paintings, films, photos and sketches. (p91)

Musée BELvue Take a trip through Belgian history. (p98)

Best Speciality Museums, Bruges

Kantcentrum Quaint lace museum where you can see the stuff being crafted. (p31)

Museum voor Volkskunde An appealing folk museum in an old *godshuis* (almshouse). (p30)

Choco-Story All you ever wanted to know about chocolate. (p35)

't Begijnhuisje Peek inside a typical old *begijnhof* home. (p50)

Frietmuseum Only in Belgium: a celebration of chips. (p35)

Diamantmuseum Lots of sparklers, and diamond-polishing demos. (p55)

Best
Parks & Gardens

The cities' parks and gardens offer more than a breath of fresh air; they're also oases of art, history and culture. The big smoke, Brussels, is greener than you might expect, with parks right in the heart of the city plus forest on the outer fringes. Bruges has some beautiful parks lining its waterways, including one dotted with working windmills.

LONELY PLANET/GETTY IMAGES ©

Brussels Parks

The most popular of Brussels' parks – attracting everyone from lunching office workers to joggers and pram-pushing parents – is the Parc de Bruxelles. In the shadow of the Palais Royal and the Palais de la Nation, this gracious former hunting ground was laid out in the 18th century, and was the scene of bloody fighting in 1830 during Belgium's bid for independence. Near the EU, the vast Parc du Cinquantenaire is ringed by museums. At the city's southeastern edge, the wooded parkland of the Bois de la Cambre, sprawls to meet the forest of the Forêt de Soignes, while in the city's northwest, the chestnut- and magnolia-shaded Parc de Laeken extends to the Atomium.

Best Green Spaces

Parc du Cinquantenaire Green space surrounded by top museums. (p108; pictured)

Parc Léopold Take a leafy break in the heart of the EU area. (p115; Brussels)

Parc de Bruxelles One of the capital's prettiest parks. (p99; Brussels)

Minnewater Secluded paths wind around Bruges' 'Lake of Love'. (p56; Bruges)

Begijnhof The peaceful courtyard is dotted with daffodils in spring. (p50; Bruges)

Koningen Astridpark Attractive park named after the Swedish wife of King Léopold. (p130; Bruges)

Best
For Kids

WIBOWO RUSLI/GETTY IMAGES ©

The exquisite chocolate boutiques and the comic museum might be aimed squarely at adults, but little visitors will still get a kick out of visiting these two cities. Travelling between the cities is a cinch; train journeys starting after 9am are free for kids under 12, accompanied by an adult.

Kiddie Practicalities

Many B&Bs and hotels have baby cribs, but it's a good idea to reserve these as places often have just one on hand. Think twice about bringing a stroller, however, as you'll be wrestling it up and down endless flights of stairs and negotiating narrow footpaths and cobblestones. Dining with kids is rarely a problem, even at top-end establishments, but you'll never see Belgian kids running amok, and you will be expected to make sure that yours aren't either. Restaurants often have high chairs, and sometimes special children's menus, but it's worth confirming in advance. With waffles and fries proliferating throughout both cities, you may be in for a bit of arm-twisting, but kids won't go hungry.

Best for a Rainy Day, Brussels

Centre Belge de la Bande Dessinée Temple to all things Tintin. (p68)

Théâtre Royal de Toone Fabulous and traditional puppet theatre. (p83)

Best for a Rainy Day, Bruges

De Striep A comic-book cornucopia, great for kids. (p61)

Diamantmuseum Older children might enjoy the diamond-polishing sessions. (p55)

Best of the Rest, Brussels

Manneken Pis Nothing will cheer up grumpy kids like the peeing boy. (p72; pictured)

Jeanneke Pis If that doesn't work, try his female counterpart. (p72)

Le Village de la Bande Dessinée Tuck in at this cartoon-bedecked cafe. (p100)

Mural-spotting Take the kids on a cartoon-mural themed walk (p73).

Musée des Sciences Naturelles Walk with the dinosaurs at this stunning museum. (p113)

Best
Architecture

Bruges and Brussels both present a compelling cross-section of architectural styles – indeed, the fabulous architecture is the reason many visitors are here. The country's most bizarre building, the Atomium, captures the futuristic style of the dawn of the space age. Contemporary architecture has lagged behind (evidenced by the nondescript glass office blocks in the EU quarter of Brussels), but a few ground-breaking buildings are rising on the skyline, such as Bruges' red-brick concert hall, the Concertgebouw.

Architectural History

Medieval architecture – the columned Romanesque and more angular Gothic – was followed in the 16th and early 17th centuries by Flemish baroque (also known as Flemish Renaissance), inspired by flamboyant trends from Italy. The most famous examples are the gorgeous guildhalls on Brussels' Grand Place, which were rebuilt in this style following the city's bombardment in 1695.

Art Nouveau & Beyond

The late-19th-century introduction of art nouveau has left a lasting mark, especially in Brussels. This elegant style was introduced by Victor Horta, whose work is showcased at his former home, the Musée Horta. Signature motifs of sinuous swirls and floral tendrils are ubiquitous throughout Brussels, though the style would have left more of a mark had it not been for the wave of demolitions in the mid-20th century. The destruction of Horta's Maison du Peuple – torn down in 1965 to make way for an unutterably bland office building – sparked outrage, leading to the introduction of laws protecting the city's heritage.

☑ **Top Tip**

▶ Get up close and personal with Brussels' architecture with the resident-run heritage conservation group, ARAU (p116), which runs excellent coach trips (€19) taking you into buildings that are often otherwise off-limits. Book direct or through the tourist office.

Best Art Nouveau Buildings, Brussels

Musée Horta The master architect's sublime self-designed home. (p121)

Old England Building Gorgeous old department store, now housing a music museum. (p93; pictured)

Galeries St-Hubert (p75), Brussels

Centre Belge de la Bande Dessinée Housed in a gorgeous Horta building. (p68)

Falstaff Enjoy a beer in this bar designed by Houbion. (p79)

Maison Cauchie Art nouveau glamour in the EU district. (p109)

Best Churches, Brussels

Église Notre Dame du Sablon Medieval gem above a lovely square. (p96)

Cathédrale des Sts-Michel & Gudule Grand cathedral in the style of Paris' Notre Dame. (p96)

Église Notre-Dame de la Chapelle The oldest church in the capital. (p97)

Best Churches, Bruges

Jeruzalemkerk Dramatically modelled on the Church of the Holy Sepulchre in Jerusalem. (p34)

Onze-Lieve-Vrouwekerk Huge 13th-century church with a Michaelangelo statue. (p53)

St-Salvatorskathedraal Vast ancient church containing brasses and artworks. (p53)

Best of the Rest, Brussels

Grand Place Ringed by splendid gabled guildhalls. (p66)

Galeries St-Hubert Glamorous glass-covered shopping arcade. (p75)

Palais de Justice Monumental and brooding law courts. (p97)

Berlaymont Building Star-shaped building housing EU commissioners. (p115)

Best of the Rest, Bruges

OLV-ter-Potterie Baroque church-hospital complex. (p34)

Concertgebouw Bruges' dramatic concession to modernity. (p58)

Best
Festivals & Events

Not even the notoriously fickle climate can rain on Belgium's parade when it's time to party. Brussels and Bruges each host a slew of diverse events, especially midyear. And the short distances between the cities means you're only a train ride away from some sort of festivity. In addition to the tourist offices' websites, a good place to find out what's on is *Agenda* (www. brusselsagenda.be), a lively events magazine published weekly in English, French and Dutch. Many festival dates vary from year to year; check the websites for details.

Party All Night

One of the annual highlights in Brussels is the **Nuit Blanche** (www.brusselsinternational.be) in September. The idea is borrowed from Paris and has spread globally: for one 'white night', the capital stays up until sunrise, laying on a swath of events, including projections, installations, circus acts and parties, blues and more in Brussels' Jardin Botanique.

Procession of the Holy Blood

A unique and ancient Bruges event is the **Heilig-Bloedprocessie** (www.holyblood.com) on Ascension Day, when a phial of what is said to be Christ's blood is paraded through the town accompanied by dance groups, floats and actors. It's by far the city's biggest and most important festival, with up to 3000 participants and 30,000 to 45,000 spectators every year.

Best Festivals for Music

Ars Musica (www.arsmusica.be; Brussels; ⊘Mar) Audiences get wired into the contemporary music scene at this accessible festival.

Brussels Jazz Marathon (www.brusselsjazzmarathon. be; Brussels; ⊘May) Get bussed free to 125 gratis city-wide concerts, featuring 400-plus artists over three jazz-fuelled days in late May.

Les Nuits Botanique (lesnuits.be; Brussels; ⊘May) Twelve days of rock, reggae, ska, hip hop, electro, folk, rap, blues and more in Brussels' Jardin Botanique.

Ommegang procession, Brussels

Couleur Café Festival (www.couleurcafe.be; Brussels; ⊙Jun) Performers at this three-day world music and dance knees-up in late June have included James Brown and UB40.

Musica Antiqua (www.festival.be; Bruges; ⊙Aug) This festival of early music not only includes concerts but hands-on workshops such as harpsichord maintenance.

Best Festivals for Food & Drink

Choco-Laté (Bruges; ⊙Apr) Some years see a small chocolate market, others a full-blown festival with everything from tastings to chocolate beauty treatments, chocolate-and-wine pairing and a 'kids village'.

Belgian Beer Weekend (www.weekenddelabiere.be; Brussels; ⊙Sep) The Grand Place is overtaken by a veritable village of stalls selling beer and associated paraphernalia (glasses, coasters etc). Drink prices are reasonable and entry is free.

Best of the Rest

Ommegang (www.ommegang.be; Brussels; ⊙Jul) Dating from the 14th century, this medieval-style procession kicks off from the Place du Grand Sablon, ending with a dance in the illuminated Grand Place.

Brussels Summer Festival Free 10-day bash packing in more than 140 different performances (concerts, children's theatre and more), including lots of local acts. (www.bsf.be; Brussels; ⊙Aug)

Comics Festival (comicsfestivalbelgium.webnode.com; Brussels; ⊙Oct) Rub shoulders with the artists and writers behind some of Belgium's best-known comic characters.

Best
Tours

Best Bus & Boat Tours

Brussels by Water

(📞02-201 10 50; www.brusselsbywater.be; Quai des Péniches 2b; trips from €10; Ⓜ Ribaucourt) A unique and unexpected way to see Brussels is from the water. A variety of educational tours explore the canal, which cuts through the city, and there are also cruise options with live music and a drink thrown in.

Brussels City Tours

(📞02-513 77 44; www.brussels-city-tours.com; Grasmarkt 82; adult/child/concession €31/16/28; 🕙10am; Ⓜ Gare Centrale) The Grand City Tour covers everything from the Atomium to the EU, and includes some lovely art nouveau houses. You kick off with a walking tour of the Grand Place, and are then transported by coach.

Best Bicycle Tours

Brussels Bike Tours

(📞0484 89 89 36; www.brusselsbiketours.com; tour incl bicycle rental €25; 🕙10am & 2pm Apr-Oct) These four-hour tours (maximum group size 12) start from the Hôtel de Ville (Grand Place). Many first-time visitors love both the ride and the beer- and frite-stops along the way (food and drink costs extra). Beware: there are some steep streets en route.

Quasimundo Bike Tours

(📞050 33 07 75; www.quasimundo.eu; adult/student €28/26; 🕙Mar-Oct) Explore Bruges by bike on a classic 2½-hour trip taking in narrow backstreets, the medieval walls, windmills and – of course – the canals. The four-hour 'Border by Bike' tour takes you as far as the Dutch border, via Damme, Oostkerke castle and assorted canals and windmills.

Best Specialist Tours

Horse-Drawn Carriage Tours

(per carriage for a 30min tour €39; 🕙9am-early evening, depending on demand) Touristy and

SIRA ANAMWONG/SHUTTERSTOCK ©

☑ **Top Tip**

Pick up USE-IT's free leaflet for self-guided walking tours off the beaten track in Brussels.

cheesey it might be, but you'll learn a lot about Bruges from the carriage tours, and there's an undeniable charm to exploring the cobbled lanes and canals the old-fashioned way.

USE-IT Tours

(📞02-218 39 06; use.it.travel/cities/detail/brussels; Galerie Ravenstein 17; 🕙10am-6.30pm Mon-Sat; 🛜; Ⓜ Gare Central) Free informal tours of different Brussels neighbourhoods, focussing on street life and society rather than history, depart from the office in Ste-Catherine.

Survival Guide

Survival Guide

Before You Go

When to Go

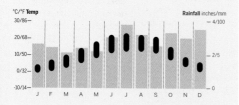

°C/°F Temp
30/86—
20/68—
10/50—
0/32—
-10/14—

J F M A M J J A S O N D

Rainfall inches/mm
— 4/100
— 2/5
— 0

➡ Winter (Nov–Feb)
Short, cold days with occasional snow. Museums and attractions are quieter, and prices are generally lower. A good time to visit Bruges.

➡ Spring (Mar–May)
Cold to mild; often wet and blustery. Major sights start getting busier; parks and gardens begin to blossom.

➡ Summer (Jun–Aug)
Weather mainly sunny, though it may rain at times. Main tourist season. A great time for music festivals.

➡ Autumn (Sep–Nov)
Mild, mixed weather. Good for exhibitions and the arts.

Book Your Stay

➡ Brussels abounds with accommodation options, including over 14,000 hotel rooms. Most are geared for midweek Eurocrats, which means there are often astounding deals for tourists, especially on weekends.

➡ Top-end hotels often charge extra for breakfast on weekdays, but throw in lavish weekend buffets.

➡ Some midrange and top-end establishments also slash their rates during the summer holidays (roughly mid-July to mid-September).

➡ Bruges is the exact opposite of Brussels: hotels are packed and prices tend to be higher on weekends. Book well ahead for high season (approximately Easter to late October) and for December's Christmas markets.

seful Websites

onely Planet (www.nelyplanet.com/hotels) uthor-penned reviews f Lonely Planet's top hoices.

ed & Brussels (www.bnb-russels.be) Many B&Bs in ruges and Brussels can e booked through Bed Brussels, which also of-ers various packages.

isitBrussels (visitbrus-els.be) Reservations can e made for free via the russels tourist office ebsite.

Hostelling International HI; www.hihostels.com) For ooking HI hostels.

est Budget

aptaincy Guesthouse www.thecaptaincybrussels. om) A warm-hearted ndependent hostel in a 7th-century Brussels mansion.

Bauhaus (www.bauhaus. e) Bruges' backpacker village, a self-proclaimed egend.

2go4 (www.2go4.be) Bar-gain dorms and doubles n the heart of Brussels.

Bruegel (www.hihostels. com/hostels/brussels-bruegel) Good location on the edge of the Marais in Brussels.

Best Midrange

B&B Huyze Hertsberge (www.bruges-bedandbreak-fast.be) Soothing pale colours and a great canal-side location in Bruges.

B&B Dieltiens (www.bedandbreakfastbruges.be) Amazingly affordable rooms in the heart of Bruges.

Chambres en Ville (www.chambresenville.be) Fantas-tically elegant rooms and studios in Brussels.

Chambres d'Hôtes du Vaudeville (www.theatre-duvaudeville.be) Classy B&B with an incredible location right within the gorgeous (if reverberant) Galeries St-Hubert in Brussels.

Best Top End

Relais Bourgondisch Cruyce (www.relais-bourgondischcruyce.be/) Luxurious little boutique hotel occupying a unique part-timbered medieval house in Bruges.

Guesthouse Nuit Blanche (www.bb-nuitblanche.com) Utterly romantic 15th-century Bruges house filled with antiques.

Dukes' Palace (www.hoteldukespalace.com) Imposingly tall with a Disney-esque turret, this five-star hotel partly occupies Bruges' 15th-century royal palace.

Hôtel Métropole (www.metropolehotel.com) Marbled opulence round every corner in this Brus-sels hotel.

Hôtel Le Dixseptième (www.ledixseptieme.be) A hushed magnificence greets you in this alluring boutique Brussels hotel.

Arriving in Bruges & Brussels

☑ **Top Tip** For the best way to get to your accommodation, see p80.

Brussels Airport

➡ **Brussels Airport** (www.brusselsairport.be) is 14km northeast of the city; the arrivals hall (Level 2) has a moneychanger (but watch the rates), car-rental agencies and tourist information. The bus terminus and luggage lockers are on Level 0, the train station is on Level 1.

➔ Airport City Express trains run four times hourly between Brussels Airport and the city's three main train stations, Bruxelles-Nord (15 minutes), Bruxelles-Central (€8.50, 20 minutes) and Bruxelles-Midi (25 minutes). Express bus 12 links the airport to Bruxelles-Luxembourg via Nato HQ and Metro Schuman (prepurchased/bought-aboard €3/4). It should take around 30 minutes, but allow much more at rush hour. After 8pm at weekends, the slower route 21 is substituted. See www.stib.be for the rather complex timetables.

➔ MIVB/STIB (www.stib.be) runs express buses (line 12 on weekdays, line 11 on weekends) from the airport to Schuman metro station and then on to Gare Bruxelles-Luxembourg. The service runs regularly from 7am to 8pm (outside these hours and on weekends Schuman is the last stop)

taking roughly 30 minutes. Tickets cost €3.

➔ A taxi to central Brussels will cost aroun €38.

Brussels South Charleroi Airport

➔ Brussels' second airport, **Brussels South Charleroi Airport** (www.charleroi-airport.com), is 46km southeast of the city and is used mainly by budget airlines, including Ryanair.

➔ Buses to Brussels Bruxelles-Midi, from which you can connnect to the metro, leave around half an hour after flight arrivals (€14; one hour).

➔ The airport also has direct bus services to Bruges four times per day (€20/38 one-way/return; two hours).

Bruxelles-Midi

➔ The **Eurostar** (www.eurostar.com) whisks you between Brussels' Bruxelles-Midi and central London's St Pancras International Station in just one hour, 51 minutes.

➔ There are two trains an hour from Brussels to

Bruges (from €19 one-way; 50 minutes).

Bruges Railway Station

Bruges' train station is 1.5km south of Markt.

There are regular buses into town, or you'll easily find a taxi.

Twice-hourly trains run to Brussels via Ghent. Hourly trains go to Antwerp, Knokke, Ostend and Zeebrugge via Lissewege.

Getting Around

Bicycle

☑ **Best for**... making like a local.

Villo! (☎078-05 11 10; en.villo.be; subscription per day/week €1.60/7.65) is a system of 180 automated stations for short-term bicycle rental in Brussels. First you need a subscription, then charges accumulate and are debited from your credit/bank card.

Tickets & Passes in Brussels

➡ In Brussels, transport tickets are valid for one hour and are sold at metro stations, STIB/MIVB kiosks, newsagents and on buses and trams.

➡ Single STIB/MIVB tickets cost €1.80 including transfers, while unlimited one-day passes cost €6. Note that airport buses are excluded and slightly higher 'jump' fares apply if you want to connect to city routes operated by De Lijn (Flanders bus), TEC (Wallonia bus) or SNCB/NMBS (rail).

➡ Children under six travel free.

➡ Tickets must be validated before travel, in machines located at the entrance to metro platforms or inside buses and trams. Travelling with an unvalidated ticket will incur a fine; random checks are made.

➡ In Brussels, bicycles can be carried on metros and trams except at rush hours (7am to 9am and 4pm to 6.30pm), once you've purchased a one-year bike pass (€15).

➡ Bruges is a great city for cyclists – it won't take you long to get anywhere, even to the coast, by bike.

➡ For bike rental in Bruges, including tandems, try **Eric Popelier** (☎050 34 32 62; www.fietsenpopelier.be; Mariastraat 26; per 1 hr/half-/full day €4/8/12, tandem €10/17/25; ☺10am-6pm).

➡ Take a trip with **Brussels Bike Tours** (☎0484 89 89 36; www.brussels-biketours.com; tour incl bicycle rental €25; ☺10am & 2pm Apr-Oct). The tour (maximum group size 12) starts from the Hôtel de Ville (Grand Place).

Boat

☑ **Best for**... Bruges romantics.

➡ Boats in Bruges depart roughly every 20 minutes from the jetties south of the Burg, including Rozenhoedkaai and Dijver.

➡ Tours last around 30 minutes (adult/child €7.60/3.40).

➡ Expect queues in summer.

Tram, Premetro & Bus

☑ **Best for**... outlying areas in Brussels.

➡ Brussels' vast web of bus and tram transport has no central hub, so grab a free STIB/MIVB transport map before going too far.

➡ Underground premetro trams link Brussels-Nord (Gare du Nord) and Brussels-Midi (Gare du Midi) via the Bourse.

Dos & Don'ts

➡ Brussels is bilingual, but in Bruges you should speak English rather than French.

➡ When meeting for the first time, men and women, and women and women, greet each other with three kisses on the cheek (starting on the left): after that it's usually just one kiss (on the left). Men meeting men generally shake hands.

➡ Trains run every 10 to 15 minutes.

➡ Public transport in Brussels runs from 6am to midnight, after which it's taxi only except on Friday and Saturday, when 17 Noctis night-bus routes (€3 one-way) operate twice hourly from midnight to 3am, most starting from Place de Brouckère.

Car & Motorcycle

☑ **Best for**... independence.

➡ Public transport is the easiest way to get round Brussels: the slightest hiccup brings traffic to a halt, especially on Friday afternoons.

➡ In Brussels, street parking requires meter-payment when signs say *betalend parkeren/ stationnement payant* (usually 9am to 1pm, and 2pm to 7pm Monday to Saturday).

➡ Major car-rental companies have offices at Bruxelles-Midi and Brussels Airport, but rentals from their downtown premises usually cost less. Try **Avis** (☏02-537 12 80; www.avis.be; Rue Américaine 145; ☒93, 94) or **Budget** (☏02-646 51 30;

www.budget.be; Hotel Bristol Ave Louise 91; ☒93, 94).

➡ Given central Bruges' nightmarish one-way system, the best idea for drivers is to use the large covered car park beside the train station, which is reasonably priced.

Taxi

☑ **Best for**... late nights.

➡ Official taxis (typically black or white) charge €2.40 pick-up, plus €1.80/2.70 per kilometre within/outside Brussels. There's a €2 supplement between 10pm and 6am. Waiting costs €30 per hour.

➡ Taxes and tips are officially included in the meter price, so you should ignore requests for extra service charges.

➡ Taxis in Brussels wait near the three central train stations; outside Hôtel Amigo, near the Grand Place; and at Place Stéphanie on Ave Louise.

➡ Cabbies have a reputation for aggressive, over-fast driving but if you're seriously dissatisfied you can report them toll-free on ☏0800 940 01 – the receipt, which they must legally print for you,

hould have their four-
igit taxi ID.

▶ In Brussels, try **Taxis
Bleus** (☎02-268 00 00;
ww.taxisbleus.be) or **Taxis
Verts** (☎02-349 49 49;
ww.taxisverts.be).

▶ In Bruges, taxis wait
on the Markt and in
ront of the train station.
Otherwise you can phone
☎050 33 44 44 or
☎050 38 46 60.

Essential Information

Business Hours

☑ **Top Tip** Post offices
generally operate from
9am to 5pm Monday
to Friday and until
noon Saturday. Smaller
branches close for lunch;
larger ones stay open
until 6pm.

Reviews in this book
won't list business
hours unless they vary
significantly from these
standards.

▶ **Banks** 9am to 3.30pm

▶ **Brasseries** 11am to
1am

▶ **Cafés** 10am to 5am;
closing times usually

depend on how busy a
place is on any given
night

▶ **Restaurants** 11.30am
to 3pm and 6.30pm to
11pm

▶ **Shops** 9am to 6pm
Monday to Saturday;
some also open on
Sunday

Discount Cards

▶ Save a bundle with
the **Brussels Card** (www.
brusselscard.be; 24/48/72hr
€22/29/35) or **Bruges
City Card** (bezoekers.
brugge.be/bruggecitycard;
48/72hr €46/49) – they
give discounts at some
concert venues, restau-
rants and bars, and save
you money on transport.

▶ Many of Belgium's
attractions and enter-
tainment venues offer
discounts for students
and children; family rates
are rare.

▶ Students will need to
produce an International
Student Identity Card
(ISIC) to qualify for
reduced admission and
discount cinema tickets
and train fares.

▶ Senior citizens and
travellers with disabilities
will generally receive a
discount.

Electricity

230V/50Hz

Emergency

**Ambulance/
Fire Brigade** ☎100

Helpline ☎02-648 40 14
Brussels-based 24-hour
helpline.

Police ☎101

SOS Viol ☎02-534 36
36 Rape crisis line in
Brussels.

Money

▶ **ATMs** Widely available
in Brussels and Bruges.

▶ **Currency** Belgium uses
the euro (€). For updated
currency-exchange rates,
check www.xe.com.

Money-Saving Tips

➡ Both cities offer useful discount cards for museums, transport and eating and entertainment discounts.

➡ On the first Wednesday of the month, many Brussels museums are free from 1pm.

➡ The **Arsène office** (☎02-512 57 45; www.arsene50. be; Rue Royale 2; ⏰12.30-5.30pm Tue-Sat; Ⓜ Parc) at the tourist office in Brussels offers heavily discounted tickets for cultural events.

➡ Food markets in both cities offer great supplies for self-caterers at reasonable prices.

➡ **Credit cards** Visa is the most widely accepted credit card, followed by MasterCard. American Express and Diners Club cards are only accepted at the more exclusive establishments.

➡ **Moneychangers** There are exchange bureaus (*wisselkantoren* in Dutch, *bureaux d'échange* in French) at airports or train stations as well as major tourist precincts. Few establishments accept travellers' cheques.

➡ **Tipping** Tipping is not obligatory, as service and VAT are included in hotel and restaurant prices. It's common to round up restaurant bills and taxi fares by a euro or two. In public toilets people are expected to tip the attendants (€0.30 to €0.50).

Public Holidays

New Year's Day
1 January

Easter Monday
March/April

Labour Day 1 May

Ascension Day
40th day after Easter

Whit Monday
7th Monday after Easter

Festival of the Flemish Community 11 July

Belgium National Day
21 July

Assumption Day
15 August

All Saints' Day
1 November

Armistice Day
11 November

Christmas Day
25 December

Safe Travel

➡ While the rate of violent crime in Belgium is low compared with many European countries, petty theft does occur, more so in larger cities. Pickpocket haunts in Brussels include the Grand Place, the narrow streets around Ilôt Sacré, Rue Neuve, and the markets at Bruxelles-Midi and Place du Jeu-de-Balle

Telephone

Mobile Phones

➡ Belgium uses the GSM 900/1800 cellular system, compatible with phones from the UK, Australia and most of Asia (and all tri-band phones), but not with GSM 1900 phones from North America or the separate Japanese system.

Phone Codes

➡ Belgium's international country code is ☎32. Area codes for each city are incorporated into telephone numbers. You must dial the area code, even when dialling from within the relevant area. Telephone numbers given in this book include the necessary area codes.

Making International & Domestic Calls

→ Public telephones that accept stored-value phonecards (available from post offices, telephone centres, newsstands and retail outlets) are the norm.

→ You can use Skype to call internationally at internet cafes, and at the computer terminals of some hostels.

Useful Numbers

Directory assistance (English-speaking operator) ☏ 1405

International dialling code ☏ 00

International operator ☏ 1324

Toilets

→ Public toilets are generally clean and well looked after. You'll be given a foul look or reprimanded if you attempt to leave without tipping the attendant (€0.30 to €0.50); this goes for both men and women.

Tourist Information

☑ **Top Tip** The superb free USE-IT guide-maps are full of spot-on local tips and irreverent humour.

Brussels

→ **Visit Brussels** (Map p70; ☏ 02-513 89 40; http://visitbrussels.be; Rue Royale 2; ⏱ 9am-6pm Mon-Fri, 10am-6pm Sat-Sun; M Parc) has stacks of excellent Brussels-specific information; there is another branch at the **Grand Place** (Map p70; ☏ 02-513 89 40; visitbrussels. be; Hôtel de Ville, Grand Place; ⏱ 9am-6pm; ᮁ Bourse).

→ **USE-IT** (Map p70; ☏ 02-218 39 06; use-it.travel/ cities/detail/brussels; Galerie Ravenstein 17; ⏱ 10am-6.30pm Mon-Sat; 🛜; M Gare Central) Friendly youth-orientated tourist office; it also does free alternative city tours.

Bruges

→ Bruges' main tourist office, **In & Uit Brugge** (Map p52; ☏ 050 44 46 46; www. brugge.be; 't Zand 34; ⏱ 10am-6pm Mon-Sun) is located inside the contemporary, redbrick Concertgebouw (Concert Hall).

→ There is also a smaller branch inside the train station (10am to 5pm Monday to Friday, to 2pm Saturday and Sunday).

Travellers with Disabilities

→ **Taxi Hendriks** (☏ 02-752 98 00; www.hendriks.be) in Brussels have taxis that can accommodate wheelchairs.

→ Some public buildings have lifts and/or ramps, but the majority don't. Outdoors, wheelchair users are up against uneven cobblestones, narrow pavements and steep kerbs. When travelling on the national railway, wheelchair users must give an hour's notice. Currently, only a handful of Brussels' metro stations have lifts (elevators), though Brussels' new leather-seated trams, which are currently being rolled out, are wheelchair accessible.

Visas

→ There are no entry requirements or restrictions on EU nationals visiting Belgium.

→ Citizens of Australia, Canada, Israel, Japan, New Zealand and the USA do not need visas to visit the country as tourists for up to three months.

→ Except for nationals from a few other European countries (such as Norway), everyone else must have a visa – check with Belgium's **Ministry of Foreign Affairs** (diplomatie.belgium.be) for info.

Language

Belgium's population is split between Dutch-speaking Flanders (*Vlaanderen* in Dutch) in the north and French-speaking Wallonia (*la Wallonie* in French) in the south, as well as a small German-speaking region in the east.

If you spend any time travelling around Belgium, you'll have to get used to switching between Dutch (*Nederlands*) and French (*français*). Bruges in the north is Flemish and therefore Dutch-speaking. Brussels is officially bilingual, though French has long been the city's dominant language.

Most of the sounds used when speaking both French and Dutch can be found in English. If you read our pronunciation guides below as if they were English, you'll be understood just fine.

To enhance your trip with a phrasebook, visit **lonelyplanet.com**. Lonely Planet iPhone phrasebooks are available through the Apple App store.

French – Basics

Hello.
Bonjour. — bon·zhoor

Goodbye.
Au revoir. — o·rer·vwa

How are you?
Comment allez-vous? — ko·mon ta·lay·voo

I'm fine, thanks.
Bien, merci. — byun mair·see

Please.
S'il vous plaît. — seel voo play

Thank you.
Merci. — mair·see

Excuse me.
Excusez-moi. — ek·skew·zay·mwa

Sorry.
Pardon. — par·don

Yes./No.
Oui./Non. — wee/non

Do you speak English?
Parlez-vous anglais? — par·lay·voo ong·glay

I don't understand.
Je ne comprends pas. — zher ner kom·pron pa

French – Eating & Drinking

A coffee, please.
Un café, s'il vous plaît — ewn ka·fay seel voo play

I'm a vegetarian.
Je suis végétarien/ végétarienne. (m/f) — zher swee vay·zhay·ta·ryun/ vay·zhay·ta·ryen

Cheers!
Santé! — son·tay

That was delicious.
C'était délicieux! — say·tay day·lee·syer

Please bring the bill.
L'addition, s'il vous plaît. — la·dee·syon seel voo play

French – Shopping

I'd like to buy ...
Je voudrais acheter ... — zher voo·dray ash·tay ...

I'm just looking.
Je regarde. — zher rer·gard

How much is it?
C'est combien? — say kom·byun

t's too expensive.
'est trop cher.   say tro shair

an you lower the price?
ous pouvez   voo poo·vay
aisser le prix?   bay·say ler pree

rench – Emergencies

lelp!
u secours!   o skoor

:all the police!
ppelez la police!   a·play la po·lees

:all a doctor!
ppelez un   a·play un
nédecin!   mayd·sun

'm sick.
e suis malade.   zher swee ma·lad

'm lost.
e suis perdu/   zhe swee·pair·dew
erdue. (m/f)

Vhere are the toilets?
Où sont les   oo son lay
oilettes?   twa·let

rench – Time & Numbers

Vhat time is it?
Quelle heure   kel er
st-il?   ay til

t's (eight) o'clock.
' est (huit)   il ay (weet)
neures.   er

t's half past (10).
' est (dix) heures   il ay (deez) er
t demie.   ay day·mee

morning	matin	ma·tun
afternoon	après-midi	a·pray·mee·dee
evening	soir	swar
yesterday	hier	yair
today	aujourd'hui	o·zhoor·dwee
tomorrow	demain	der·mun

Monday	lundi	lun·dee
Tuesday	mardi	mar·dee
Wednesday	mercredi	mair·krer·dee
Thursday	jeudi	zher·dee
Friday	vendredi	von·drer·dee
Saturday	samedi	sam·dee
Sunday	dimanche	dee·monsh

1	un	un
2	deux	der
3	trois	trwa
4	quatre	ka·trer
5	cinq	sungk
6	six	sees
7	sept	set
8	huit	weet
9	neuf	nerf
10	dix	dees
100	cent	son
1000	mille	meel

French – Transport & Directions

Where's ...?
Où est ...?   oo ay ...

What's the address?
Quelle est l'adresse?   kel ay la·dres

Can you show me (on the map)?
Pouvez-vous   poo·vay·voo
m'indiquer   mun·dee·kay
(sur la carte)?   (sewr la kart)

I want to go to ...
Je voudrais   zher voo·dray
aller à ...   a·lay a ...

What time does it leave?
À quelle heure   a kel er
est-ce qu'il part?   es kil par

Dutch – Basics

Hello.
Dag./Hallo.   dakh/ha·loh

Goodbye.
Dag.   dakh

How are you?
Hoe gaat het   hoo khaat huht
met u?   met ew

Fine. And you?
Goed. En met u?   khoot en met ew

Please.
Alstublieft.   al·stew·*bleeft*

Thank you.
Dank u.   dangk ew

Excuse me.
Excuseer mij.   eks·kew·*zeyr* mey

Yes./No.
Ja./Nee.   yaa/ney

Do you speak English?
Spreekt u Engels?   spreykt ew *eng*·uhls

I don't understand.
Ik begrijp het   ik buh·*khreyp* huht
niet.   neet

Dutch – Eating & Drinking

I'd like the menu, please.
Ik wil graag   ik wil khraakh
een menu.   uhn me·*new*

What would you recommend?
Wat kan u   wat kan ew
aanbevelen?   *aan*·buh·vey·luhn

Delicious!
Heerlijk!/Lekker!   heyr·luhk/le·kuhr

Cheers!
Proost!   prohst

Can I have the bill, please?
Mag ik de   makh ik duh
rekening   rey·kuh·ning
alstublieft?   al·stew·*bleeft*

breakfast	*ontbijt*	ont·beyt
lunch	*middagmaal*	mi·dakh·maa
dinner	*avondmaal*	aa·vont·maa
beer	*bier*	beer
bread	*brood*	broht
coffee	*koffie*	ko·fee
fish	*vis*	vis
meat	*vlees*	vleys
nuts	*noten*	noh·tuhn
red wine	*rode wijn*	roh·duh weyr
tea	*thee*	tey

Dutch – Shopping

I'd like to buy ...
Ik wil graag ...   ik wil khraakh ...
kopen.   koh·puhn

I'm just looking.
Ik kijk alleen maar.   ik keyk a·*leyn* maar

How much is it?
Hoeveel kost het?   hoo·*veyl* kost huht

That's too expensive.
Dat is te duur.   dat is tuh dewr

Can you lower the price?
Kunt u wat van de   kunt ew wat van duh
prijs afdoen?   preys af·doon

Do you have any others?
Heeft u nog   heyft ew nokh
andere?   an·duh·ruh

Dutch – Emergencies

Help!
Help!   help

Leave me alone!
Laat me met rust!   laat muh met rust

Call the police!
Bel de politie!   bel duh poh·*lee*·see

Call a doctor!
Bel een dokter!   bel uhn *dok*·tuhr

I'm sick.
Ik ben ziek.   ik ben zeek

I'm lost.
Ik ben verdwaald.   ik ben vuhr·*dwaalt*

Where are the toilets?
Waar zijn de   waar zeyn duh
toiletten?   twa·*le*·tuhn

Dutch – Time & Numbers

What time is it?
Hoe laat is het?   hoo laat is huht

It's (10) o'clock.
Het is (tien) uur.   huht is (teen) ewr

Half past (10).
Half (elf).   half (elf)
(lit: half eleven)

morning	*'s ochtends*	sokh·tuhns
afternoon	*'s middags*	smi·dakhs
evening	*'s avonds*	saa·vonts
yesterday	*gisteren*	khis·tuh·ruhn
today	*vandaag*	van·daakh
tomorrow	*morgen*	mor·khuhn
Monday	*maandag*	maan·dakh
Tuesday	*dinsdag*	dins·dakh
Wednesday	*woensdag*	woons·dakh
Thursday	*donderdag*	don·duhr·dakh
Friday	*vrijdag*	vrey·dakh
Saturday	*zaterdag*	zaa·tuhr·dakh
Sunday	*zondag*	zon·dakh

1	*één*	eyn
2	*twee*	twey
3	*drie*	dree
4	*vier*	veer
5	*vijf*	veyf
6	*zes*	zes
7	*zeven*	zey·vuhn
8	*acht*	akht
9	*negen*	ney·khuhn
10	*tien*	teen
100	*honderd*	hon·duhrt
1000	*duizend*	döy·zuhnt

Dutch – Transport & Directions

Where's ...?
Waar is ...?   waar is ...

What's the address?
Wat is het adres?   wat is huht a·*dres*

Can you show me (on the map)?
Kunt u het   kunt ew huht
mij tonen   mey *toh*·nuhn
(op de kaart)?   (op duh kaart)

Please take me to ...
Breng me   breng muh
alstublieft naar ...   al·stew·*bleeft* naar ...

What time does it leave?
Hoe laat   hoo laat
vertrekt het?   vuhr·*trekt* huht

A ticket to ..., please.
Een kaartje naar   uhn *kaar*·chuh naar
... graag.   ... khraakh

I'd like to hire a bicycle.
Ik wil graag   ik wil khraakh
een fiets huren.   uhn feets *hew*·ruhn

Index

See also separate subindexes for:

⊗ **Eating p173**

⊙ **Drinking p173**

⊛ **Entertainment p174**

⊕ **Shopping p174**

Behind the Scenes

Send Us Your Feedback

We love to hear from travellers – your comments help make our books better. We read every word, and we guarantee that your feedback goes straight to the authors. Visit **lonelyplanet.com/contact** to submit your updates and suggestions.

Note: We may edit, reproduce and incorporate your comments in Lonely Planet products such as guidebooks, websites and digital products, so let us know if you don't want your comments reproduced or your name acknowledged. For a copy of our privacy policy visit lonelyplanet.com/privacy.

Helena Smith's Thanks

Continued thanks to Anne Ponslet, Kristof Buntinx and the USE-IT gang. Also to Karel for the hospitality.

Acknowledgements

Cover photograph: A canal in Bruges, Belgium, Alan Copson/AWL.

Photograph on pp4-5: Cafes and restaurants on Markt square, Bruges, Glenn Van Der Knijff/Getty Images.

Brussels Transit Map ©STIB/MIVB 04/2015

This Book

This 3rd edition of Lonely Planet's *Pocket Bruges & Brussels* guidebook was researched and written by Helena Smith. The previous editions were written by Helena Smith and Catherine Le Nevez.

This guidebook was produced by the following:

Destination Editor
Kate Morgan

Product Editor
Sarah Billington

Senior Cartographer
David Kemp

Book Designer
Wibowo Rusli

Assisting Editor
Kate Evans, Simon Williamson

Cover Researcher
Naomi Parker

Thanks to
Wayne Cardozo, Kate Chapman, Ryan Evans, Andi Jones, Wayne Murphy, Catherine Naghten, Karyn Noble, Kirsten Rawlings, Paul Snell, Angela Tinson, Tony Wheeler, Mirjam Zdybel

Our Writer

Helena Smith

Helena fell for Brussels on a drunken/architecture week
end with a great friend; she goes back for the live music
the chocolate and the vampires. A travel writer and
photographer, Helena blogs about food and community
at eathackney.com.

Published by Lonely Planet Publications Pty Ltd
ABN 36 005 607 983
3rd edition – April 2016
ISBN 978 1 743210 000
© Lonely Planet 2016 Photographs © as indicated 2016
10 9 8 7 6 5 4 3
Printed in Malaysia